ERRATA PUBLISHING A BOOK IN A COVID WORLD:

As a result of enforced delays and restrictions in the printing process due to the COVID pandemic , several footnotes were omitted in printing this book. They are included here for your reference:

From page 100.
Footnote 70

A very fine book that gives a great summary of these three views and an excellent response to inclusivism is Christopher W. Morgan and Robert A. Peterson, eds., *Faith Comes by Hearing: A Response to Inclusivism* (Downers Grove, IL: InterVarsity Press, 2008). Some use the term "universalism" (which suggests that all will ultimately be saved) and "pluralism" (as defined here) interchangeably. See page 6 of Morgan & Peterson.

Footnote 72

James Borland, "A Theologian Looks at the Gospel and World Religions." *Journal of the Evangelical Theological Society* 33 (March 1990), p. 3–11.

Footnote 73

Morgan and Peterson, *Faith Comes by Hearing*, p. 36.

From page 123
Footnote 98

The book was *Creative Counterpart* by Linda Dillow. For many years, *Partenera Creatoare* (Creative Counterpart) was the only Christian book explicitly for women in Romania. The English version of this book is available today on Amazon as *Creative Counterpart: Becoming the Woman, Wife, and Mother You've Longed to Be* (Nashville, TN: Thomas Nelson, 2003). It has been in print since 1977, and close to half a million copies in English have been sold around the world. No one knows how many copies have been printed in Romanian, Hungarian, and other Eastern European languages since it first appeared in the early 1980s. Today the book's name is *Partenera Creativă* (Creative Partner) in Romania. Stories are told of how the book was copied by hand during the eighties to present to couples before their wedding. Linda Dillow and her books are still much loved in Romania, across Eastern Europe, and around the world. Linda was among the travellers who came from Vienna to teach women's groups during the eighties.

What Others Are Saying About *reGeneration*

Through rich storytelling, Miriam Charter ushers us into the mysterious world of international work. She captures the imagination through harrowing tales and then infuses them with theoretical perspectives from history, missiology, and theology. Story and theory work together to assist and challenge the reader in working through dilemmas anticipated by those who will be working in hard places. With generosity of spirit and risky vulnerability, she shares stories that read like an informal conversation between a seasoned international worker and the next generation of internationally curious students. Further conversations will be ignited, especially among those who are considering going to hard places.

—Pam Nordstrom, Ph.D.
Provost, Vice President Academic
Ambrose University, Calgary

The author spent an intrigue-filled decade working in communist Romania. An unexpected and invaluable outcome of that solid contribution is the amazing yet simple discipleship model that was put into motion. While many churches today struggle to find and then implement an effective way to disciple believers, Dr. Charter, although working in a hostile environment, managed to set in motion a self-perpetuating disciple multiplication model based on 2 Timothy 2:2. Seeing this astounding result, along with her ever-developing and doctrinally sound convictions, makes this book a truly compelling and instructive read.

—Ron Brown, D. Min.
Former international worker with the Christian & Missionary Alliance in Canada

In a masterful way, the author draws you into a missional drama that reads like a spy novel. Secret meetings in secret places with a sacred agenda—how to reach people with the Good News of Jesus in very dark and challenging places? On the loom of the written page, the author delicately weaves together theological truth and compelling stories that both intrigue and inspire. She artfully creates space for deep reflection and at the same time releases fresh imagination. This is a powerful and prophetic call to courageously step into the hard places of this world to bring access to Jesus. Do you feel the tug to engage? Lean in and let the adventure begin!

—David Hearn, D.Min.
President of the Christian & Missionary Alliance in Canada

This book reads like a spy novel, yet Miriam Charter experienced it all. She vividly recaptures the years she regularly crossed the border into communist countries to serve the underground church by teaching the Bible. But *reGeneration* is much more than a great story. Miriam challenges a new generation to take God's Word to hard places in our world. Her experiences and her honest questions open surprising concerns requiring careful Biblical analysis—an analysis which does not disappoint. We recommend this book as an *essential* read to educate missionaries who will in turn commit the Word *"to faithful people"* (2 Timothy 2:2, NET) in other cultures.

—Duane Elmer, Ph.D., and Muriel Elmer, Ph.D.
Educators and cross-cultural trainers
Trinity Evangelical Divinity School, Deerfield, IL (retired)
Authors of *The Learning Cycle: Insights for Faithful Teaching from Neuroscience and the Social Sciences* (IVP, 2020)

If you are a citizen of the world with a heart for the nations, and love a good story, you are going to thoroughly enjoy reading this book. Miriam Charter (Distinguished Alumna of 2012) has gathered these stories from her life in China and Eastern Europe. The stories are riveting, reflecting the real-life tension of building the Kingdom of God in hostile environments. As an added bonus, Miriam unpacks and attempts to resolve some of the ethical dilemmas that naturally occur in that context. May you sense the heart of our loving Father for the nations of the world as you read this record of his work in enemy territory.

—Mark L. Maxwell
President
Prairie College, Three Hills, AB

reGeneration is an inspiring collection of stories about men and women standing for the gospel at a time in the twentieth century when they could have been imprisoned, tortured, and even killed for their faith. Written by a person who was actually there, this book is a must-read for those drawn to cross-cultural communication and mission. Dr. Charter demonstrates the necessity of mission *with* over against mission *to* another people. She is candid about her difficulties in "becoming one" with the people of Romania, and humble in the recounting of God's extraordinary protection—even the unmistakable intervention of angels.

—Linda Cannell, Ph.D.
Academic Dean (retired) at North Park Theological Seminary, Chicago, IL

I met Miriam in 1986, in a small apartment in Romania. A group of seven or eight Christian women were there. It was a dark, cold, winter evening—but the first time such a group of women had gathered to study. We were so excited! Miriam opened a window for us to see the garden of our faith, beliefs, and life principles. And now this book brings back that view, seen through the window *and* from walking on the path of the garden. A great journey!

—Mirela Rădoi DeLong
Editor-in-Chief
Logos Publishing House, Romania

Not many Christians make history and then write history. As a passionate historian of Protestant missions in Romania, I am really pleased to read Miriam's stories of leadership training behind the Iron Curtain. She returned to Romania after 1989, not only to continue to work, but to evaluate the results of that risky investment, and also to document the history of the underground ministry in which she was involved. This kind of work must be brought to light, not only because it is still almost unknown and undocumented, but it has a powerful motivational potential for a church brutally thrown, in just a few years, into a society dominated by materialism, consumerism, and denial of Christian values. *reGeneration* is a well-documented and well-written book which should be on the reading list of those who are passionate about the Great Commission, looking for inspiration to see how to get involved in ministry in an increasingly hostile environment for Christian witness.

—Mihai Ciuca
Journalist and church historian
Romania

reGeneration is written for everyone who is called by God—male or female, married or single, young or old—to accomplish God's purpose in this broken world. We call it missions. In this book, Dr. Charter unfolds her stunning story of missions in the communist world with valuable lessons learned from her own experience. Her insights provide not only an understanding about the reality and complexities involved in the life of international workers in hard places, but also challenge the reader about the necessity of entrusting the body of faith to the next generation.

—A.N. Lal Senanayake, Ph.D.
Director/President, Lanka Bible College and Seminary, Sri Lanka

In a sense, there are no "easy places" for mission outreach today. Every area has difficult challenges in our unsettled world. Miriam Charter has served in the hardest places and has seen how God does the unusual in hostile places. This book will instruct and inspire a new generation preparing to serve, and will be a valuable resource for cross-cultural teaching and learning. It will be an encouragement for experienced missionaries as well. Here we have the opportunity to learn from Miriam's rich experiences as a missionary, scholar, professor, mentor, and minister. Dive into it!

—James E. Plueddemann, Ph.D.
Chair of the Missions Department at Trinity Evangelical Divinity School,
Deerfield, IL (retired)
International Director of SIM (retired)
Author of *Teaching Across Cultures* (IVP, 2018)

When asked to list Scripture verses that deal with the Great Commission, many—maybe most—Christians would list Matthew 28:19–20, followed by an embarrassed silence. Yet, from God's covenant to bless all nations through Abraham to Jesus' last command to go into all the world and preach the gospel, the "Great Commission" runs like a spinal cord through Scripture. Miriam Charter's book, an exquisite combination of theology and practice, concept and story, joy and sorrow, local and global, individual and corporate, is a worthy companion for any pastor who wants to fulfill his call to build a global impact church that faithfully engages in this Great Commission.

—Sunder Krishnan
Pastor of Rexdale Alliance Church (Etobicoke, ON) for thirty-six years (retired)
Author of *Hijacked by Glory: From the Pew to the Nations* (2014)

This book will be a helpful resource for professors of mission, pastors of mission, and all who are involved in preparing the next generation of international workers for challenging places in the world. I would especially recommend this book to women who are willing to face down danger for the sake of the Kingdom, and to churches who will affirm, resource, and walk with them as they take the gospel to those places where it has yet to be fully been established, through discipleship and leadership development.

—Mary Cloutier, Ph.D.
Associate Professor of Intercultural Studies
Moody Bible Institute and Moody Theological Seminary, Chicago, IL

Modeling the power of story, Miriam addresses important and perplexing issues in modern missions. Her incredible, faith-building tales from communist Romania—including efforts to outwit the secret police by flushing away a memorized travel itinerary, encounters with angels, and eye-witness accounts of unbearable suffering for followers of Jesus—challenge the reader to take seriously the church's mission to take the gospel to hard places. The book is a valuable tool for those who "feel the tug of the nations"—those who will go, and those who will walk with them in support—as they, together, pass their faith on to the next generation.

—Lisa Rohrick
. Canadian Pacific District Mission Mobilizer
Christian & Missionary Alliance in Canada

Miriam is a great storyteller. Her content is fascinating! Amazing stories about God's presence, protection, and provision among his people who served in a hard place—communist Romania in the eighties. There is always hope even for the darkest situation. God keeps working through his servants who are willing to obey his calling at all costs! These inspiring, firsthand stories presented with solid theoretical foundations will bring strong encouragement for those who are called to serve in hard places of the world, local or international workers alike.

—Sutrisna Harjanto, Ph.D.
Principal of Bandung Theological Seminary, Indonesia

My generation, the millennial generation, is often seen as primarily driven by purpose. And while this book is a must-read for everyone regardless of age, it is especially imperative for all millennials and Gen Zers—from those who may be searching to know their purpose to those who need to be reminded of the unique design with which God has created them. We know God's grander plan to reconcile the whole world to himself, but we sometimes struggle to see exactly where or how we fit into it. Miriam's wisdom and captivating stories will help you along the path to discovering your piece of the puzzle and how it fits into the "hard places" where God lives, and where he invites us to join him.

—Matt Chan
Postsecondary advancement professional
University of Calgary

Today, international mission work is promoted through slick videos, understood (poorly) through two-week short-term engagements, marred by colonialist labels, or considered an endeavour reserved for the radical. Miriam Charter's book instead makes mission *personal* and *honest*. Her deeply reflective stories of living the gospel truth in the challenging years of communist Europe in the 1980s will help you, and those you may be coaching toward a cross-cultural mission life, understand that while the commitment to crossing culture is definitely challenging, the God who crossed into the world through Christ is already there at work. She'll help you see just how possible it is for you to join Him.

—Harv Matchullis
Director, Candidate Recruitment & Development Office
The Alliance Churches of Canada

This book is a testament to God's work in the "hard place" of Romania. We feel Miriam's passion for the unreached, the wide-ranging impact of a clandestine disciple-making program among women, and her heart for the next generation to whom she passes the baton. Our world has significantly changed, but now with more opportunities and unique challenges. Many hard places remain. Miriam's stories enlarge our vision for mission and will serve as a beacon and inspiration for present and future international workers!

—Joanna Feliciano-Soberano, Ph.D.
Academic Dean, Asian Theological Seminary, Manila, Philippines
Overseas Council Regional Director for Southeast Asia

This book is a reminder of the grand mission of the church to reach the least reached and unreached for Jesus. As a seasoned educator, pastor, and international worker, Miriam speaks a fresh authentic word to which the church does well to listen. Well-told stories and missiological principles clearly expressed. Should be read by every serious follower of the Way!

—Gordon Fowler
Lead Pastor during the 1970s at Foothills Alliance Church, Calgary, AB

Could what happened forty-two years ago, when church elders identified Miriam's calling to unreached people, be the norm today? Foothills Church has designated this book as a *Legacy Project*, a written record of our vision to mobilize the next generation of international workers, and those who will serve the churches here in North America who send them. This book will be a helpful tool for local churches like ours to use in equipping the rising generation of IWs. It will deeply inspire all who embrace the call of Jesus to the nations.

—Ian Trigg, D.Min.
Lead Pastor
Foothills Alliance Church, Calgary, AB

God has established his church in the world for the purpose of making Christ's disciples of all peoples. He calls individuals to this work, sends them to places near and far, and sustains them when they face hardships. Are you worried about security and safety in times of uncertainty in your participation in God's mission? Read Miriam Charter's book and you will find encouragement in her stories and lessons. A significant contribution.

—Tite Tiénou, Ph.D.
Research Professor, Theology of Mission,
and Dean Emeritus, Trinity Evangelical Divinity School, Deerfield, IL

reGeneration

STORIES OF RESILIENT FAITH IN COMMUNIST ROMANIA

"Let the nations be
glad and sing for
joy!" Ps. 67:4

M Charter

Miriam Charter

FOREWORD BY MARK BUCHANAN

REGENERATION
Copyright © 2020 by Miriam Charter

Printed in Canada

Print ISBN: 978-1-4866-2069-2
eBook ISBN: 978-1-4866-2070-8

Word Alive Press
119 De Baets Street, Winnipeg, MB R2J 3R9
www.wordalivepress.ca

MIX
Paper from
responsible sources
FSC® C016245

Cataloguing in Publication may be obtained through Library and Archives Canada

To the women of Romania
my daughters in faith

I have no greater joy than to hear that my children are walking in the truth.
—3 John 1:4

Contents

In Gratitude

The pages of this book are filled with true stories about real people who changed my life. I'm so grateful for friends in Romania who gave me time during three months of research in 2018 and 2019. You drove me from city to city, hosted me in your homes, and fed me favourites like *sarmale* and *salată de vinete*—oh yes, and *raclette*! You confirmed or corrected my memories of our experiences during the decade I shared with you in communist Romania. Your names are too numerous to list.

Thank you to my extended family, to friends on every continent, to life-long mentors who have spoken into my life and into this book, to doctoral students who serve with distinction in challenging places around the world. I think of you as the "cloud of witnesses" about whom Hebrews 12:1 speaks. Some are already cheering from heavenly places; others regularly cheer me on by WhatsApp or email!

I reserve profound thanks for my dear friend Willie Murray, who can no longer understand when I thank him for his role in my life and in this book, though I told him many times before clarity began to fade. In the summer of 1982, very last minute, Willie asked me to substitute for him as an instructor at a short-term mission training conference in Pennsylvania, even offering me some of the notes he had already prepared before he had to cancel. He allowed me to take his notes and make them my own. His thoughts on the ethics of ministry in countries that seem closed to the gospel form the basis of what I write in Chapter 3. While in Pennsylvania I met Tom Lewis, who introduced me to the ministry this book is about, BEE (Biblical Education by Extension). I write about him in Chapter 1. Tom is now cheering from heaven. For these godly men who invested in me, I will be forever grateful.

Thank you to Ron Brown, who sat with me at Denny's in June 2018 and dreamed up the idea of this book, as only Ron can do! He suggested it be not simply a book of stories, but that it might also include lessons that will be important for the next wave of international workers. Our shared passion for the nations, his reading of multiple drafts of the manuscript, and his unrelenting belief in the book have sustained the process.

I am grateful to those who read early drafts of the manuscript and gave helpful, constructive feedback: Lynda Brown, Myra Brown, Ron Brown, Linda Cannell, Matt Chan, Dora Dueck, Eleanor Fowler, Gordon Fowler, Lisa Hines, Cyndy Ingram, Nathan Kinnie, Sandi Kinnie, Myrna McCombs, Lisa Rohrick, Ruth Shareski, Lisa Sung, Karen Vine, Hannah Wollin, Rob Wollin, and Brian Buhler (who also provided a theological critique).

I am very thankful for the support of everyone at Word Alive Press throughout the publishing process. I offer special thanks to Matthew Knight, whose gracious work as editor shepherded *reGeneration* to publication. His work was meticulous but never mechanical—he always preserved my voice in the text. I'm grateful.

It would take pages to list all who prayed for and encouraged me while I was doing research in Romania, and those who invested in the Legacy Project which Foothills Alliance Church established to finance my research trips. Your names would fill pages. Many of you prayed even as the events of this book unfolded in the 1980s. Back then, I called you my "Inner Circle." You've never abandoned your dual role of prayer and financial support for me over thirty-seven years. You believe in me. The Ladies' Afternoon Prayer Group at First Alliance Church has prayed for me for nearly forty years. Your persistent prayers have been the wind beneath my sails. As you, one at a time, are joining the cloud of witnesses in heaven, I wonder who in the next generation will take your places. Perhaps I will.

Thank you to those who wrote endorsements for the book: pastors, international workers, former doctoral students, former faculty colleagues at Trinity Evangelical Divinity School and Ambrose University, and colleagues in the Christian and Missionary Alliance. And to Mark Buchanan, who wrote the Foreword. Mark immediately *got* the book when I spoke about it because he, too, is building into the next generation—especially writers! Thank you, Mark, for picking me up and putting me back on the wagon!

For all of you I am grateful.

Foreword

To meet Miriam Charter, you might not at first take her for a trapeze artist. And, well, she's not.

But in a way, she is: trapeze artist, and international treasure hunter, and code-breaker, and spy, and revolutionary. She's performed some of the most daring high-wire acts and leaps in mid-air I've ever seen, and most without a net beneath her. She ranks as one of the bravest people I know, with a fierce unbending unrelenting readiness to go to almost any length to complete her mission.

So let me call her what she actually is: Missionary. And storyteller. And teacher.

And this is her story—part memoir, part call to arms. Prepare in these pages to meet a woman whom the Apostle Paul would easily recognize as a kindred spirit. Miriam takes us behind the Iron Curtain in one of its worst incarnations, Romania in the 1980s (as well as a few other communist states in that period). She smuggles us, hair standing up on end, past border guards and secret police and suspicious taxi drivers and the ever-present "Boris," and whisks us straight into the bleak heart of one of history's most repressive regimes. And there, at the very centre of all that bleakness and darkness and danger, she unveils a light so bright, so defiant, so re-demptive, no force, human or demonic, can squelch it.

It's the church living out the gospel.

Reading this, at times you won't know if you're rollicking your way through a Tom Clancy novel or reading a missionary biography, but here's a way to tell: the novel is easier to put down.

Yet Miriam more than entertains. Throughout her story, she stops, steps back, and distills into nuggets the crucial lessons she's learned from her holy skullduggery. But even this has a larger purpose: she's heaven-bent on inspiring and helping the next generation to go, go now, go into all the earth, go to the very ends of the earth, go and fearlessly be and share good news with those who have yet to hear it, or have heard only a partial or skewed version of it. She does this—this work of inspir-ing—not by painting a picture of how exotic or thrilling it all will be, but quite the opposite: how flat out difficult and bone-rattling frightening it often is. This going will land you in hard places, and confront you with excruciating dilemmas—that is, when it's not sticking you in the mud of endless tedious governmental bureaucracy and incompetence and corruption.

And yet.

And yet, reading Miriam's story gave me one overriding emotion: envy. How I wish I had in my lifetime taken more risks for the gospel. How I wish I had lived my life more fully and courageously.

But it also gave me another strong emotion: desire. How I long to do so now.

—Mark Buchanan
Author of *God Walk: Moving at the Speed of Your Soul* (2020)
Teaches Pastoral Theology at Ambrose Seminary, Calgary

Map of Romania

Preface

Whatever you heard me teach before an audience of witnesses, I want you to pass along to trustworthy people who have the ability to teach others too.
—2 Timothy 2:2, VOICE

If you take the Great Commission of Jesus seriously, this book is for you. If you feel the tug of the nations*[1] on your heart every time you watch the evening news, your concern for unreached people who have not yet heard the Good News might increase as you read this book.

Thirty-five years ago, I was an international worker* in communist Europe. Every few years I returned to Canada, telling stories to anyone who would listen about the price people paid to follow Jesus in countries like Romania, Bulgaria, and Russia. Today, I meet people in their thirties or forties who were children back then. They remember my stories with amazing clarity. They always ask, "Have you written a book with those stories in it yet?" They want their children and grandchildren to hear what I told them. They were the inspiration for me to start writing this book.

First of all, this is a book of true stories from communist Europe in the 1980s. But it's much more than that. These stories illustrate mission dilemmas I faced in those years, real-life situations that happened because I was working in a hard place. New recruits who go to the nations today will similarly find themselves in hard places, dealing with some of the same things I had to go through. Two thousand years ago, Jesus told His followers to *"go and make disciples of all nations"* (Matthew 28:19–20). During the past two hundred years, thousands of courageous men and women have stepped up to take the gospel to unreached people.* Some people call these recent centuries the "great missionary era." The places they went to were hard places. And yet I'm tempted to say that the "easy places" have been reached. I'm not diminishing in any way the sacrifices made to take the gospel around the world in the last two centuries. But the craziness of today's world makes me wonder if, by

---

1   The first use of a term defined in the Glossary on pages 161–163 is marked with an asterisk*.

comparison with Romania in the eighties, the places yet to be reached will be even harder. If you are among the next wave of international workers, the people you eventually go to will live in places or cultures that make them really hard to reach. Or it could be that just by listening to the story of Jesus, the people you talk with will be introduced to a life of suffering. Obeying God's call will probably land you, and them, in a really hard place.

My hard place in mission was communist Romania in the 1980s. Christians were under attack by a militant regime that wanted, more than anything else, to wipe out God's church—send it into extinction. They tried hard, as hostile governments still do today, hoping that if they could extinguish just one generation of believers—silence them, stomp out the embers—momentum would be lost, the movement would soon die, and Christians would become extinct.

But a regenerative process was set in place in the early eighties in Romania. Groups of pastors, and soon thereafter, groups of women, realized that if they passed their faith to the next generation, and in turn, the next generation passed it to the next, and the next passed it to the next... the flames of faith could never be extinguished. It would be a never-ending reGeneration of faith. The growth of faith would be exponential. Instead of extinction, a movement of resilient faith was set in motion that still burns today, forty years later.

This book is for the next generation of international workers who will take the Good News to hard places in the world. I want to contribute something very tangible to your passionate following of Jesus. I want to help you think through situations you might encounter in your life on mission.

This book is also written for many people in God's church—people of all ages who love their international workers but might never leave home themselves. This group includes enthusiastic young adults whose hearts have been captivated on a short-term mission trip to some place where following Jesus is just stinkin' hard. This group includes elderly women who have loved on and prayed faithfully for their international workers (they still call them *missionaries*) for decades. These wonderful women know more than most about what it means to work in a hard place because, by prayer, they've walked with IWs in those places. This group includes professional men and women who work in the downtown core, or tradespeople who support and cheer on international workers. They finance God's mission in hard places, sometimes making significant sacrifices to do so.

What do all of these people in the church have in common? Several things. They love IWs. They are learners. They want to better understand what it means to live and work in a hard place. They want to grow in their understanding of missional* issues. They want to learn how to speak more effectively into the lives of those the church sends. They are absolutely the best cheerleaders of international workers. This book of stories and lessons is also for them.

Each chapter is a set of stories that point to one of seven lessons I learned as my years in communist Europe unfolded. Each chapter begins with a story that introduces a missional issue. Story is a powerful way to learn. To help the reader engage with the issue before moving on to the next section of the chapter, there are a few questions that might help you reflect on what you already know about the missional topic being introduced. These questions are called Time to Reflect. You might reflect by yourself or with a discussion group that shares your interest in mission. In the next section in each chapter, Going Deeper, you will learn about the issue from the perspective of theology, history, or missiology.* Each chapter concludes with a few more stories from my own experience of the specific issue. At the end of the chapter is a section called Going Further: Recommended Reading. I will suggest one or two of the best resources I know on the topic discussed in the chapter.

A few of my stories come from my childhood in the early days of communist repression in China, but most of them come from communist Romania and Russia. As I write, my mind reaches back thirty-five years to people of faith who showed me what it means to live obediently in the face of determined efforts by a regime to extinguish faith. They were resilient. Resilience is the capacity to recover from harsh blows and unspeakable suffering. Their faith was resilient as they trusted the Lord of the church who promised to build his church, even in hard places. That hard place was Romania in the 1980s.

Romanian Christians from the 1980s have very important things to say to the rest of the Christian world. Their stories need to be told to two groups: to the next generation of international workers who will take the Good News to people who have never heard of Jesus, and to those who will stay at home to mobilize and care for the ones who go.

I tell their stories with much delight. We can learn a lot from them—that is why I wrote this book.

Prologue

Servants in High Places

I always looked forward to visiting Titus and Victoria in Zalau (Zalău).[2] Foreign tourists weren't allowed to travel to the Romanian city of Zalau during the 1980s. After all, what tourist would choose to visit such an ugly factory town? Its muddy streets were lined with grey, cinder-block apartment buildings constructed to enable Nicolae Ceausescu (Ceauşescu)'s[3] plan to resettle millions of farmers to the cities for factory jobs. That was the dictator's grand scheme of *modernization*, his attempt to transform Romania from an agricultural economy to an industrial one.

In the minds of the authorities, there was nothing of interest for tourists in this city. They suspected that foreign travellers, if they dared to visit Zalau, had intentions other than tourism. So the secret police hung around the train station, studying the faces of all who descended from the trains, determined to keep people like me from seeing the harshness of life in a place like this. We had to develop ways of getting in and out of the city without being noticed.

The authorities were confounded by the boldness of Pastor Titus, who travelled from village to village to care for eighteen churches. They tried to limit his ministry by taking his driver's license from him for minor, trumped-up driving infractions, or by limiting his gas ration to fifteen litres a month. Both restrictions made it hard for him to serve so many village churches, spread all over the countryside as they were.

His family was also often the target of attempts by the government to end his ministry. Titus and Victoria were forced to sell their home and furniture to pay a fine of 7000 lei* that the authorities levied against the church for what they called "building illegally," when, after fifteen years of being refused a permit to build, the church members began to do so anyway. For several years, the family of five lived in

---

2   The first time a Romanian personal or place name appears, the Romanian spelling (if there is one) will be indicated in parentheses. Each time after that, only the English spelling will be used.

3   This name is approximately pronounced "Chow-uh-shes-koo."

rooms at the back of the church, sleeping on mattresses on the cold cement floor. Victoria cooked for them on a stove in a shed behind the building.

The winter of 1986 was particularly cold. The authorities limited electricity for a family to forty-two kilowatts a month. In those days, most of Romania's power was exported to the Soviet Union, one of the dictator's many schemes to eliminate the national debt. The common citizen paid the price for this indignity. On the radio, people heard the constant propaganda commanding them to "conserve, conserve, conserve electric power." Space heaters weren't allowed in homes. Titus and Victoria, whose three rooms at the back of the church were cold and drafty, far exceeded their ration for electricity. As a result, their power was cut for four days during the most bitter days of the winter of 1986.

Being a man of courage, Titus went to the utility office to plead the welfare of his young children. He was told that someone would come to reconnect their power. When the man descended from the pole, having reconnected power to their humble church "home," he whispered to Titus, "Use all the power you wish, as I've put the meter on a much slower rate. It will take a long, long time for you to use forty-two kilowatts."

With a grin, Titus told me the story and whispered, "God has his servants in high places, even among officials in the utility office in Zalau!"

Romania in the 1980s

The 1980s was one of the darkest decades in the history of the church in Romania. In fact, the decade was punishing for all Romanians, but especially for followers of Jesus. These were the years I worked in Romania, and the period of time in which my stories take place. Return trips to Romania in 2018 and 2019 allowed me to interview pastors about the cruelty of the 1980s. They agreed it was an especially dark time for the church. Under the cruel dictator, Nicolae Ceausescu, the communist government made life for those who followed Jesus almost unbearable.

Ordinary citizens lived under the watchful eye of the ubiquitous and brutal secret police* force. The Securitate[4]* tried to minimize contact between citizens and travellers from the West for two reasons. First, they wanted to control what Westerners learned about life under Ceausescu. They were afraid tourists would tell Western media the truth about Romania. Second, they wanted to limit what local citizens learned about life in the West, because such information might incite rebellion. Ordinary Romanians were fearful to confide anything of substance to a

---

4   The terms "secret police" and "Securitate" are used interchangeably throughout the book.

foreigner, which made us wonder if we understood even a small part of what they really suffered. People would whisper Ceausescu's name, knowing well the penalty for criticizing the government. No one was ever sure, but everyone assumed that their homes were bugged* and that even conversations in the street were potentially being recorded with listening devices. Every typewriter had to be registered yearly so the government could trace letters exposing the truth about life in Romania that had been written by journalists or academics to places like Radio Free Europe or BBC Radio. Owners of typewriters would have to annually type a test page for police records, allowing authorities to discover the source of any undesirable writings intercepted in the mail according to the unique imprint of each typewriter.

The harshest brutalities were reserved for Christians who bravely resisted the regime's attempts to silence them and destroy the church. The vascular surgeon who translated for me one day in Braila (Brăila) told me that as soon as he made public his decision to follow Jesus, he was brought before a crowd of five hundred medical professionals whose task it was to publicly humiliate him. The possession of Bibles or Christian literature from the West was a criminal offence. My friend, Constantin, was sentenced to seven years in prison because Bibles were found in his car. The husband of a woman in one of my groups, an elder in his Baptist church, was sent by the authorities to a psychiatric hospital for "rehabilitation." He died there several months later from a "medical" injection that killed him, believed to be the work of the secret police. In every denomination, schools for pastoral training were either closed or limited to a handful of students each year. Ceausescu's Ministry of Cults exercised rigid control over every aspect of pastoral education: curriculum, faculty, who was accepted to study, and even the placement of graduates in churches.

My Life in Romania
My experience of the Romanian church in the 1980s was up close and personal. I worked in the underground church* for most of the eighties, observing firsthand the price believers paid to live faithfully for Jesus. In those days, Western travellers like me couldn't get visas to live in Romania. It was possible to get a tourist visa, but purchasing one meant that you were followed by the secret police night and day.

Our hotel rooms were bugged. We always acknowledged "Boris," the unseen presence in our hotel rooms who listened in on every conversation, day and night. We were aware of the microphones implanted by the Securitate in flower vases in hotel rooms and in ashtrays on certain restaurant tables that were reserved for Westerners only. We would move the ashtray to a nearby table when we wanted a place to talk without someone eavesdropping, but it would quickly be returned to our table by the server, with the menacing warning that tableware must stay on the appointed table. We would limit conversation at that table to the tourist attractions we'd seen that day.

We spent a lot of time trying to outwit the secret police in our work with the underground church. I travelled as a legitimate representative for a travel agency in Calgary, scouting out tourist locations for high-adventure travellers.[5] It was a truthful cover that worked for a decade.

Three Data Sources

The book in your hands brings together three sources of data, the first being my experiences among Romanian Christians in the 1980s. In those years, Westerners could only engage with the church very secretively, flying under the radar of the secret police and doing everything we could to avoid bringing danger to the Christians we came to serve. Some of those stories are told in this book.

The book also draws on letters I wrote during the eighties to my family and a close group of trusted, praying friends whom I called my "Inner Circle." I lived in Vienna, Austria in those years, and like many other international workers from the West, I travelled from Vienna into Eastern Bloc* countries. I wrote long letters from Vienna after each trip, recounting the details of my adventures. When my mother died, we found the letters among her things. She had saved every single one. They are an important part of the story.

Finally, I gathered more crucial data during two return visits to Romania in 2018 and 2019—a total of three months travelling around the country and talking with Romanians about life in the 1980s. I needed to make sure that what I remembered of those days and what I had written in my letters was not exaggerated. On those trips I spoke with many of the pastors and the women I'd worked with, interviewing them and their children and other Romanians who had experienced communist Romania in the eighties. They confirmed that in the eighties their country was a "hard place"—we can safely say this decade was the worst in Romanian history. As I listened to the stories of the men and women I had worked with, I concluded they would be good examples for the next generations who will take the Good News to hard places.

I hope these stories transport you into that space in which Romanian believers in the 1980s and we who worked alongside them often found ourselves. There,

---

5   The Calgary-based travel agency saw me as a non-salaried travel researcher and gave me business cards imprinted with their address and my name. I made occasional reports on potential tourist destinations—their business card got me into many countries.

we often felt like we were caught between a rock and a hard place. But in that tight space, God, our Rock, provided everything we needed to confront the perplexing dilemmas we encountered.

Some of the dilemmas we faced on mission in those days are similar to dilemmas today's international workers will encounter as they follow God's call into other hard places in our world. I'm thinking of realities like how best to pass faith to the next generation in repressive contexts, or the sadness of knowing that people die without ever hearing about Jesus. They will deal with ethical issues that arise when they work in places where, if the government knew what they were doing, they would not approve.

Illustrations come from my experience of life under a communist regime in the darkest period of the church in Romania. A few stories are ones my parents told me about our lives in China, my birthplace, in the early days of Maoism* (1940s). I also tell one story from my life in Russia, a country that continues to be a hard place to work in.

The Story Begins

CHAPTER ONE

Bucharest, November 1983

The plane comes to an abrupt stop on the tarmac. Through the window over the wing, I catch a glimpse of a bleak, wintry landscape. The grey-green face of Otopeni International Airport, Bucharest (Bucureşti)'s most important link with Western Europe, stands in the distance. Men in long, military green wool coats, with furry army-issue hats and assault rifles slung across their chests, are scattered across the pavement. They surround the plane as it comes to a full stop. The muffled overhead announcement, first in German and then Romanian, asks passengers to remain seated until the seatbelt sign has been turned off—but no one pays any attention as they retrieve hand luggage from the overhead bins.

As I leave the Austrian Airlines jet, a world of cleanliness and order is immediately exchanged for one of black and grey images in the shivery, late-afternoon November light. Only a one-hour flight away, Vienna seems part of some distant experience. We shiver in the cold at the bottom of the stairs as a bus, which will deliver us to the terminal, lumbers toward us.

Otopeni Airport is a structure of crumbling marble and dirty glass with passport officers in what appear to be temporary plywood cubicles. A red star and a photograph of the dictator hang from the otherwise empty walls in the passport hall. I purchase a tourist visa for five days and am forced to exchange fifteen U.S. dollars for each day I will be in the country.

I remember the briefing my friend, Tom Lewis, gave me during my twenty-four-hour layover in Vienna. This trip was Tom's idea. He wanted me to explore working with an underground* pastoral training program in Eastern Europe. I think of his preparation, not even one day ago, about how to answer the question at customs as to which hotels I will stay in—a question to be answered very carefully. By law, hosting Westerners in your home is a criminal act for a Romanian citizen. The plan is that in one city I will stay in a believer's home for the night. I have reservations in hotels for all the others.

The customs hall is dark, and feels dirty and unfriendly. The official addresses me in halting Chinese when he notices in my passport that I was born in China. He gives my luggage a quick, disinterested search.

As a taxi driver leads me to his waiting car, an icy blast of wind announces that winter has arrived in Romania. We make our way down Calea Bucureștilor, the wide boulevard that connects Otopeni with Baneasa Airport, the domestic airport closer to the city. A sense of desolation settles over me—I am now ten thousand kilometres from home, and no one in the world knows precisely where I am. From the back seat, I watch the ashen, pockmarked face of the taxi driver, realizing he is checking me out in his rear-view mirror. In the streets, Romanians lean into the wind, dressed in heavy overcoats and winter hats with earmuffs and gloves, intent on getting home before dark.

As the driver navigates the tree-lined boulevard to the domestic airport, I notice the steep-roofed houses standing back from a front line of beeches, poplars, and large-leaved linden trees, their barren branches crackling and snapping in the bitter wind. I pay the taxi fare, certain he is gouging this naive Westerner who, he correctly assumes, doesn't have a clue what the thirty-minute ride is worth.

In my twenty-four-hour layover in Vienna, Tom prepared me for my five-day solo journey into communist Romania. He gave me an itinerary which he told me to memorize. I took careful notes during his briefing, writing down his directions for connecting with believers *in country*, noting how—without speaking—I would know that the person I was connecting with was legitimate.

I trust Tom's briefing, because he runs the base in Vienna and has prepared many travellers for missions to the church in Eastern Europe. Several times he reminded me that in Eastern Europe, well-made plans don't mean a whole lot! "Expect the unexpected," he cautioned me, suggesting that my hand-written notes and itinerary, once memorized, be torn up and flushed down the toilet on the flight to Bucharest. The night before had been almost sleepless as I transformed my notes for teaching into code form so they wouldn't attract attention or—worse yet—be taken from me by customs officials.

If Otopeni International Airport was bleak and dirty, it was a gentle introduction to the domestic airport, Banaesa. Built in the early twentieth century, Banaesa Airport obviously hasn't kept up with the development of business and leisure tourism in much of Europe.

A soldier unbolts the front door and allows me to enter. He re-bolts it after I am inside. My luggage and I are immediately subjected to a thorough search. Only then am I allowed to enter the main rotunda of the small airport, a space that is dark and in great disrepair, under layers of dust. A severe-looking woman sits in a roughly constructed plywood booth with a dim, exposed lightbulb hanging over her head. Her body is wrapped in a heavy black coat, which she pulls tightly around herself against the chill in the hall. I am sent back and forth between two such booths, one of them being the reservations counter and the other the place for payment.

Yes, the reservation Tom made for me in Vienna for the 4:30 flight to Oradea has found its way to some office in Bucharest. I see my name, written in pencil on a sheet of yellowed paper that has been torn from a scribbler—the only name on the page. I pay for the flight and the attendant indicates that I should put my suitcase on a grocery cart sitting nearby, an almost comical and certainly unsophisticated way of checking luggage. She tells me they will announce my flight soon.

Evening is falling quickly. No lights come on as the hall becomes increasingly gloomy. The loudspeakers in the room crackle and sometimes fade completely for seconds, mid-sentence, as muffled announcements are made. People sit around the hall on their suitcases, some on the dusty floor and some anxiously standing near the Departures door.

Fearing I might not understand the announcements being broadcast, but noticing that the language is distinctively Latin-sounding, I get up the courage to ask a beautifully groomed young woman standing near me if she speaks French. She nods, and I ask if she will alert me when the 4:30 flight for Oradea is announced. She is quick to tell me that this particular flight to Oradea, a city on the western side of the country near the border with Hungary, is often delayed or cancelled in winter because of extreme cold and dense fog.

Her next words don't instill hope: "Don't count on the flight going… it seldom does in winter."

A Change of Plans

I feel urgency rising inside me. I am scheduled to meet with a group of pastors' wives in Oradea at 5:00, though everyone knows that the 4:30 flight from Bucharest to the western side of the country, if it happens at all and is on time, will arrive at 5:30.

A thought flashes through my mind—a *Latin* language and perhaps some *Latin* personality in this laid-back people. I begin to realize how little I know about Romania or Romanians. When Tom called me while I was still in Canada, he spoke as though he was using a phone line that we both knew was bugged. He hadn't even mentioned what country I would be travelling to, simply saying, "You will fly from Vienna to the capital of the country to which you are going on Monday morning." That prompted me to dig out an atlas, find a map of Romania, and learn for the first time that Bucharest is Romania's capital.

In the years that followed I would learn that many people in North America have no clue where Romania is and very little about Romanian people. Few know that Romania is an island of *latinity* (a Latin-based language in the same family as Portuguese, Italian, and French) in a sea of Slavic countries and Slavic languages, one of the Balkan countries bullied for years by the Soviet Union. It really is quite unfair to include Romania in the singular grey mass often referred to as the "satellite states" of the Soviet Union.

Two and a half hours pass, and finally at 6:30 my newfound French-speaking friend whispers that the flight will not be going to Oradea that night. By now, the hall in which we are standing is nearly empty and dark. No lights come on as darkness descends. She helps me get a refund for my flight and asks me what I am going to do next, warning me that I'll never find a hotel in the city at this time of day.

She seems, intuitively, to understand that I am alone and unfamiliar with Romania's disintegrating economic conditions. She has correctly concluded that I will need help getting to the other side of the country, and invites me to travel with her on the night train across Romania to Oradea.

As we leave the airport, there are no streetlights, and the outline of the distant city centre is eerily dark and foreboding on the horizon. We wait in the cold of the November night for a bus to the North Train Station, from which the night train will depart. My friend tries to protect me from the howling wind that is blowing from the north. My gloves and scarf are in my small suitcase, but this is hardly the moment to try to dig them out. It is she who realizes how cold I am—and that there will be no more buses that night. It is she who hails a taxi which deposits us thirty minutes later at the Gara de Nord train station. It is she who buys my ticket for Oradea (first class, so she says) and leads me to the Salle d'Attente (waiting room) to wait for an hour till the night train leaves.

The dimly lit waiting room is filled with gypsies,*[6] and the air hangs heavy with the stench of stale cigarette smoke, body odour, and sour cleaning mops. By now, I'm feeling hungry, not having eaten since the airline sandwich and cup of coffee just

---

6   In the 1980s, the term "gypsy" was not considered racist or offensive. Post-revolution, the official name became Rom/Roma rather than țigan/țigani (gypsy/gypsies). However, even today, books printed in Romania that speak of a past era continue to use the term țigan, a label that even gypsies still prefer.

before we landed at noon. I wonder out loud to my friend if I will be able to buy a meal on the train. She grimaces and quickly responds that even if there is food for purchase on the train, which there won't be, I won't want to eat it! She also tells me I cannot drink the unfiltered water from the filthy water fountain in the waiting room.

As we wait, she tells me about life in Romania's capital city. The situation is deteriorating quickly: food, fuel, water, and electricity shortages are said to be worse than during World War I. Though she and her husband are both engineers working for the Ceausescu government, there had been nothing at home that morning which she could pack to eat on this journey.

It will be twenty-six hours from the sandwich on Austrian Airlines until my next meal and a drink of bottled water.

The Night Train

It is soon time to find the platform from which the night train will leave the capital at 9:15. My friend warns me that she was unable to get seats in a non-smoking car, also apologizing for the disgusting conditions on the train.

I am glad she prepared me. A chemical stench hangs in the air as we enter our first-class compartment. The seat covers smell like they've been washed in kerosene—perhaps intended to kill unwanted little *beasts* left behind by travellers who have sat in this compartment.

As travellers pack the train, the heat increases in the compartment, as does the smell of human bodies wrapped in winter clothing. As the train pulls out of the station, the woman opposite me becomes sick as the heat and smell increase, further adding to the stench in the crowded compartment.

By now my friend has introduced herself to me as Maria. She begs me not to visit the washroom, but it is now twelve hours since I left the sweet-smelling lavatory on Austrian Airlines Flight 783. I need to go—and wish I hadn't!

Through the night, Maria and I chat in French. She seems, instinctively, to know not to ask what has brought me to Romania in winter. She tells me about life in Romania, raising a five-year-old child who goes to government daycare all day so that she and her husband, also an engineer, can work. By the time they get home to their flat every night, it's time for bed. Family time hardly exists.

When I point out the injustice of a system that mandates having children by penalizing those who don't, and then requiring that the child be raised by the regime in daycare, her sober response is simply, *"C'est la vie!"*—"That's life!" Her vacant eyes tell me that it is part of the government's master plan for raising the next generation of loyal, communist comrades. I hear about her courtship and university years, but never a word of criticism of the regime that is raising her little girl—a child into whose life she has very little input.

As the train moves west into the darkness of the Romanian night, the compartment falls silent as the other four travellers close their eyes and hope for sleep. Finally, Maria too closes her tired eyes and leaves me alone with my thoughts. It would be hard not to recognize that Maria is God's gift to guide me through my first twenty-four hours in this hard place.

Lucia Speaks

The train slows to a crawl. It is 4:15 in the morning. I realize that all hope of making connection with believers in Oradea is gone. The muffled announcement of our imminent arrival in Cluj-Napoca triggers the memory of a city name that was on the itinerary I flushed down the toilet on my flight from Vienna just fifteen hours before. I am to meet someone in Cluj later this very day.

I nudge Maria and announce that I will get off the train here. I tell her I have missed my meeting in Oradea, so it makes sense to get out in Cluj. Why continue three more hours to Oradea only to immediately turn around and come back to Cluj? All I know is that later this day I am to connect with someone here in Cluj who will lead me to a meeting with pastors who study with the underground Bible school I want to join.

Maria's whispered cry is filled with concern. She tells me that train stations are locked until 5:00 a.m., reminds me that I have no hotel to go to, that there will be no taxis at this hour of the morning, that I don't speak a word of Romanian. All true. But I lower my small suitcase from the overhead rack, hug her as I whisper *"Merci!"* and leave the compartment.

I leave the train and cross empty tracks in utter darkness. The station is pitch black. Only soldiers are on the platform. One of them unceremoniously unlocks a door into the station and leads me through to the other side and into the street. With a single word I ask him, "Taxi?" He shrugs, making no motion to help.

I flag down the first car that comes along. Opening the door, I lean into the front seat. I say the name of the hotel Maria had suggested in a questioning voice. "Napoca?" The driver motions for me to get in. We wait. Before long, another couple gets in and names the same hotel. "Napoca." So off we go.

When we arrive, the driver wakes up the clerk, who sleepily assigns me to Room 312. I can see my breath in the air. There is no thermostat in the room. I haven't slept for thirty-three hours. I fall into bed at 5:00 in the morning, sleeping in all the clothes and socks in my suitcase until 2:00 in the afternoon.

Connecting in Cluj

I wake up hungry, wondering what to do next. By now, it is twenty-six hours since I've had anything to eat or drink. I lie in bed, trying to keep warm, forming a plan. I think about the memorized instructions on the itinerary I flushed down the toilet on the plane: *In Cluj, find Piaţa Unirii, the main city square. At 5:00 p.m., stand between the Catholic church and the statue of a man on a horse. A man will meet you and tell you where the group will meet that night.*

I realize that if I miss this second contact, my trip to Romania will begin to unravel. Everything hinges on meeting up with this man on the town square in just over three hours.

By 4:30, I'm sitting in a little café from where I have a good view of the square, Piaţa Unirii. I order a coffee and a piece of bread with salty cheese and salami.

Outside, people shuffle past the café window where I sit, clutching cheap burlap carry-bags, probably hoping to find stale bread in the shops. Their faces are downcast, calculating, without emotion, as if they are struggling to master life's next catastrophe. Tom in Vienna told me there were rumours circulating that all over Romania, bread was deliberately held in bakeries for twenty-four hours before selling, so it would be stale and people would buy less.

Five minutes before the appointed hour, I walk at a leisurely rate to the appointed place between the magnificent old church and the bronze statue on the town square. My heart is pounding. If I don't look Romanian, hopefully I look like a tourist—though I realize there aren't many tourists in this cold and dismal place in December. I'm standing by a splendid statue of Matthias Corvinus, King of Hungary, mounted on his horse.

At 5:00 p.m. sharp, a man walks behind me and without stopping, whispers in English, "Go into the church and wait near the front until I come for you!"

The church provides blessed relief from the biting north wind. Within minutes, he is beside me near the altar. He tells me to follow a few feet behind him into the street. There will be a car waiting on the corner with its trunk open.

It plays out exactly as he said: following him at a distance, I see him throw his small bag into the trunk of an idling car, climb in, and motion for me to do the same. The driver nods as though he has been expecting these passengers. Without a word he drives away, going around the block several times, circling back, always looking in his rear-view mirror to make sure we aren't being followed. At last, satisfied no one has seen us get into his car, he leaves the city centre and heads down a wide boulevard that is lined on both sides with nondescript grey blocks of high-rise apartments.

Rob, the stranger who spoke to me in the church, introduces himself. He is also from the West, travelling into Romania from Vienna to teach pastors in the underground Bible school—men who otherwise would have little possibility of theological and pastoral training. Tom has connected me with Rob's group of Western teachers, who have invited me to explore the possibility of joining them. The relief of having finally made contact in this bleak and unfamiliar place, knowing that from here on I have a guide to depend on, brings tears to my eyes.

Within ten minutes, the car slows to a stop in front of a tall, ugly block of apartments. We wait until the driver receives a signal from some window high up in the building that *all is clear.* "Repede!"—"Quickly!" he whispers, urging us from the car.

We stumble up the unlit stairwell to a door standing open on the fourth floor, and are unceremoniously pulled into the apartment. The door closes quickly behind us, and without a word someone leads us deeper into the apartment, into a room that is apparently the bedroom for the whole family. Every wall is lined with beds, on which are stacked pillows and bedding. Heavy curtains are drawn over the only window in the room, and an exposed light bulb hangs from the centre of the ceiling, casting a yellow glow over everything.

Only once the bedroom door is tightly closed are we introduced in whispers to our host, his wife, and three children. The door opens every few minutes as another man arrives for the evening class. Pastors come from the area surrounding Cluj, careful not to arrive in groups, which would attract the attention of nosy neighbours who would certainly report a suspicious gathering to the secret police. Every man who enters the room that night knows the risks—it is illegal for groups of more than three or four citizens to gather for any reason. The crime of meeting with foreigners to study the Bible would be deemed by the authorities as much more serious, certainly sending any one of them, especially our host, to prison. And yet they gather.

Rob leads the men through a discussion of the Old Testament book of Hosea and then gives them an oral test on their homework. The story of Hosea, who did not divorce a prostitute wife, leads to an intense discussion about husband-wife relationships. The men cluster around Rob, asking questions about his relationship with his wife. How does he deal with arguments, and what does forgiveness in marriage look like? Sitting beside me, Lucia, the twenty-five-year-old daughter of the host, quietly translates it all into French for me.

A Prophetic Word

I sense that my presence in the room provokes curiosity, if not anxiety, in the minds of the men. I see it in their eyes when Rob explains that in Canada I am a pastor and a seminary* professor, and that on this trip I am exploring the possibility of joining the underground training program of which they are a part! The men have never met a woman who is theologically trained, and certainly no Christian who believes, apparently against the teaching of Scripture, that women can teach men. There are only men in this program.

Sitting beside me, I feel an almost audible gasp from Lucia as she learns my reason for being here. As the men return to the seminar, she begins to quietly ask direct questions in French. Rather than become a distraction, I suggest we go to the kitchen to talk.

Her mother is piling steaming cabbage rolls onto large plates for the men. My theological and pastoral career has shocked the sensitivities of Lucia, who stands beside me in the kitchen, wide-eyed with excitement. When the kitchen door swings shut, she asks breathlessly, "You went to seminary and studied the Bible with men? Miriam, these pastors cannot imagine a woman teaching them anything, especially the Bible. They will never be willing to learn from you. Why don't you do something in Romania with women?"

Lucia's mother and little sister listen as she translates our brief French discussion back into Romanian. The next morning Lucia will return to her job at the train station. It will be thirty-five years before she knows the fulfillment of those prophetic words.

Birth of a Vision

At 9:00 p.m., Lucia and her mother serve cabbage rolls, little cakes, and tiny cups of sweet Turkish coffee. The men stand in a circle, praying for God's blessing on this humble home and for protection as they leave. They embrace each other and leave two at a time, without a sound as they creep down the unlit stairwell. Most of them will drive into the night to surrounding villages, and report next morning to a factory job.

Someone gives me a ticket for the night train leaving Cluj-Napoca for Bucharest at 10:30, and a man offers to drive me to the train station. By 9:30, anxiety is rising inside me. I wonder how far away the train station is. It will take me some time to adjust to what feels like a haphazard approach to schedules. Finally, we descend the dark stairway to his old car, which is parked in the courtyard. The icy blast of wind reminds me that Romania is already in the grip of winter.

I climb into the back seat as the man tries to start the old vehicle. It wheezes, sputters, and then dies. He pumps the pedals. There seems to be no life in the car. Three men on the street surround the car, offering a push which might help to fire the ignition.

In the back seat, my eyes move from my watch to God in heaven as I pray. The driver is anxious that the men pushing the car not see the Western woman in the back seat. Before long, none of us can see out as our warm breath thickens into ice on the windows. Everyone in the car is praying silently.

The driver lays his head on the steering wheel and I hear his whispered cry, "Jesus, Jesus, Jesus!" The old car coughs and lurches forward as though life has been breathed into it. At the train station, there is no time for more than a goodbye. He whispers something that I understand to mean, "Out! Quick!"

By now, a strange mixture of jetlag, fatigue, and adventure is taking over. I sleep for a few hours as the night train to Bucharest lumbers back across the country. I awaken at 5:00 and wonder where I am. One hour later we arrive in the city. Driving through Bucharest's misty morning light in a taxi to the Park Hotel, I see people standing in the cold, clutching empty canisters and cheap burlap carry-bags. They are waiting in line for bread and fuel. There are few cars in the street, and everyone is dressed in shapeless coats and furry hats. Their bent shoulders and the plod of their gait make me think of people sent into involuntary exile—but in their own country.

Many years later, I will learn that 1981 ushered in the worst decade in Romanian history. Some have argued that the political repression was actually more suffocating in the 1950s, when the Communist Party under Gheorghe Gheorghiu-Dej tried to establish thought control over an ideologically hostile population, but Romanian historians agree that the 1980s were among the most repressive years in their history.[7] During that decade, Romanians were "reduced… to an animal state, concerned only with the problems of day-to-day survival."[8]

Making Connections in Bucharest

By now, the itinerary I flushed down the toilet during the flight to Bucharest is decidedly sketchy in my memory. All I can remember is that a contact in Bucharest

7   Robert D. Kaplan, *In Europe's Shadow: Two Cold Wars and a Thirty-Year Journey Through Romania and Beyond* (New York, NY: Random House, 2016), p. 5.

8   Dennis Deletant, *Romania Under Communist Rule* (Jassy, Romania: Center for Romanian Studies. 1998), p. 118.

will speak with me at 7:30 a.m. in the coffee shop of the Park Hotel. The details of the day will depend on my connecting with a man named George, whom Tom in Vienna told me I wouldn't miss because of his large, imposing stature.

It is just as Tom promised. At 7:30 a.m, in the hotel coffee shop, I am drinking lukewarm, black coffee to accompany bread and goat cheese when George appears. It's not hard to spot him across the room. He acknowledges me with hardly a glance as he passes me and seats himself at a table in the corner. Within minutes he approaches my table, moving the ashtray to another table, and without any introduction tells me in a low voice to take a taxi to the National Opera. He will meet up with me there. Hopefully from the Opera someone will lead us to the place where the pastors are meeting today.

My journey in the taxi is like a mini unguided tour of the once-majestic city of Bucharest, formerly called by some "Little Paris." We pass some of the most beautiful sights in the city—the Arcul de Triumf, a triumphal arch modelled after the Arc de Triomphe in Paris, and government buildings that must have once been ornate and beautiful. We drive right through the old part of the city, finally arriving at the National Opera.

George is waiting at the bus stop where the taxi stops. He tells me to follow him at a distance until we get to the Metro Station Eroilor, where we must wait. Someone will connect with us there and lead us to the meeting.

In the bitter cold of the November morning, we wait on Piața Eroilor (Heroes Square) to connect with someone we have never met, someone who will lead us to our meeting. As we wait, a man descends from a bus. His eyes connect with mine as though he knows who I am—but he doesn't stop. He walks to the end of the block, turns around, and comes back past us, not stopping, not saying a word. With his back to us, he waits for the next bus and disappears from sight.

An hour and a half later, we are still waiting in the cold. The unknown man has disappeared like a vapour, and I think I'm losing feeling in my fingers and toes. We realize that we aren't going to connect with the person who was to have been our guide.

In a nearby hotel we settle down with cups of coffee to consider our options. George remembers from a previous visit to Bucharest that there is a Baptist church in the area near the hotel where we sit. Randomly he suggests that if he can find the church, someone there might know where a meeting of pastors is scheduled for today.

An hour later, he returns, jubilant. He found the little church, and when he arrived, a prayer meeting was in progress. The men around the table were asking God to guide the foreign teachers to their meeting place. The pastor they had sent to meet us at the bus stop on Piața Eroilor told them he didn't dare connect with us. He told us later that from his home that morning he had been stalked by someone who made his following very obvious. He dared not signal us when he saw us waiting at the bus stop.

George tells me that when he walked through the door of the church on Popa Rusu Street, he felt like an actor in the biblical drama of Peter's deliverance from prison. The group was praying for the apostle's deliverance, but the maid at the door refused to believe it was Peter. The praying men around the table were equally as excited and incredulous.

George leads me through the streets in the direction of the Baptist church where the men are waiting, circling the block where the church is located several times and checking over his shoulder to be sure we aren't being followed before opening the gate on the street. He leads me back to the windowless room where six pastors, leaders in the evangelical movement in Romania, are waiting.

Hands are lifted to heaven as we walk through the door. The men offer voiceless thanks to God for his protection. They shake our hands and embrace us warmly. Immediately the men settle in for a day of teaching which is already several hours delayed. It is George for whom they waited. George explains my presence as an observer, and my keen interest to join the team one day as a teacher.

All afternoon, I watch George lead the men through the seminar. I am a silent observer as he expertly discusses the homework they have brought to class. He facilitates a discussion on the Lord's Prayer (Matthew 6:9–13) and explains the assignments for the next meeting. The men are so eager to learn. I can see in their eyes such hunger for pastoral training. Because of the repressive situation in Romania, this approach is their only hope for pastoral education.[9] Some of these men pastor as many as a dozen churches because of the shortage of leaders with biblical training.

As the afternoon unfolds, I keep asking myself if what I am seeing here is the type of ministry for which God has created and equipped me. My heart warms to what I am witnessing.

The Generational Principle Is Embraced

In the early afternoon, lunch is served by two women from a little closet behind the room where we are meeting. Over steaming bowls of cabbage soup, followed by boiled potatoes and little meat patties, I talk with the men. I sense immediately their hesitation at the idea of a woman teaching in their program. Titus, who pastors eighteen congregations in the middle of the country, warms to my suggestion that maybe it would be more feasible to begin classes with their wives. Warm enthusiasm

---

9   The pastoral training program was known in those days as BEE, Biblical Education by Extension. For a brief history of BEE, see Appendix.

infuses his comment that in his city he has eight *sisters* who already serve in his congregation, women who would be ecstatic at the idea of being trained.

The words of Lucia in Cluj, just the night before, echo in my mind: "Miriam, men in Romania cannot imagine a woman teaching them anything, especially the Scriptures. Why don't you do something with women here?"

As the women clear the dishes from the table, the men continue to discuss my potential involvement in their training program. I notice they respond more positively to the possibility of a parallel program for women. I wonder if it would be kinder to duck from the room as the tension grows around the table—even the idea of training women is new to them, and a hot topic theologically. But there is nowhere for me to escape.

They ask George about the issue. Because the discussion happens with translation to English, this allows me to experience the full force of their debate. They are wrestling to understand what Scripture says about women learning, teaching, and serving in the church. They take at face value Paul's words to Timothy, *"I don't let women take over and tell the men what to do. They should study to be quiet and obedient along with everyone else"* (1 Timothy 2:11–12, MSG). As the conversation slows, I gather courage to ask them if they would feel more comfortable with me meeting regularly with their wives in the years ahead.

The room grows silent as Dr. Nick, the obvious leader among these pastors, leans into the circle with a final and definitive comment. With both palms planted on the table in front of him and a faint grin on his face, his stature is imposing. He looks straight at me, and with warm traces of a smile says, "Train women, Miriam? You can't! They talk too much!"

The room echoes with soft but jovial laughter as all of them enjoy his words, a statement with a double meaning. Quite apart from their understanding that Scripture instructs women to be silent in the church, one of the men quickly explains to me that they worry that if women are invited to a program for women, the existence of training programs from the West might be leaked to untrustworthy people. Their primary fear is that the highly prized training of pastors might be jeopardized. Each time the circle of students with knowledge of this underground program grows, so does the danger of such information falling into wrong hands. Already, the Securitate try to intimidate the men every time they meet.

We read together from 2 Timothy 2:2, *"And the things you have heard me say in the presence of many witnesses entrust to reliable people who will also be qualified to teach others."* Again, Lucia's words from the night before ring in my ears, "Why don't you start doing something with women, Miriam?"

We examine the biblical model with which these men are already very familiar.

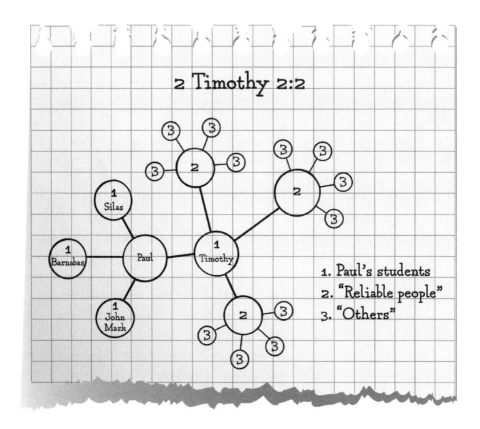

2 Timothy 2:2

I ask them to consider allowing their wives to meet with me as soon as I can relocate to Europe. Their wives will be my "first generation" of students, meeting together in secret for teaching and discipleship several times a year. I draw a crude diagram of 2 Timothy 2:2 on a page torn from my notebook and push it into the centre of the table. I put my own name in the circle at the centre of the diagram, with spokes drawn outward connecting to six circles, one at the end of each spoke. "Your wives will be my first generation of students; each of them will gather around them the second generation, a group in your home city, to whom they will teach everything I teach them. And the second generation will teach the third generation, and the third generation will teach the fourth...."

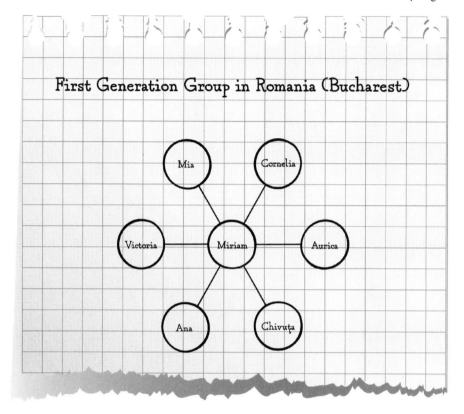

First Generation Group in Bucharest

The men nod in agreement, understanding the generational intent of 2 Timothy 2:2. I pull away from the table to allow them to discuss the outrageous idea I have just suggested. When the discussion begins to lag, I ask for a show of hands. Who will support their wives in being trained in the years ahead? Courageously, hand after hand goes up as my eyes move around those seated at the table. As each hand is raised, I ask for the name of that man's wife, which is then written in one of the first-generation circles. These men, scared as rabbits at what they are committing to, accept my invitation for their wives to become the first women's study group in Romania. With skepticism, they commit to a one-year trial.

Night has fallen. The men embrace, leaving to take night trains across the country to cities and towns where the battle with darkness rages. They depart one at a time over the next half hour. The secret police are probably sitting outside the church gate on Strada Popa Rusu, as they often do. Those who wait behind pray for the safety of their brothers now in the street.

Something new and exciting has been birthed in the hearts of these coura-geous men. As we pray together before the men leave, in my heart a conviction is growing that among women in this very hard place, an untapped resource might be harnessed for God's kingdom.

When Your Children Ask: The Power of Story

CHAPTER TWO

China 1943

Most people think of Pearl Harbor when they hear December 7, 1941, but that date makes me think of my parents' engagement. My mother and father met at Bible school in Canada in 1934 and figured that they would probably get married one day. My father went to China in 1938. He was born in China, so for him it was going home to the country and language of his childhood. Mother sailed for China in 1940, and their relationship took off through letters, even though they took months to reach each other. Take, for example, the letter in which my father proposed to my mother. He wrote from south China on the day Pearl Harbor was bombed, but the letter took months to reach her in north China, where she was in school learning Chinese.

One year after getting engaged, they began to plan their wedding in south China. But there was one big barrier to the wedding: distance! My mother lived in north China, and my father was already working among the tribal people of Yunnan province in the far south. They were separated by thousands of kilometres. A civil war was raging between the Nationalists and the Communists, who were both fighting the Japanese. That meant travel was incredibly dangerous, especially for a single woman in a country at war.

But my adventurous mother embarked on the journey from north to south, an unimaginable journey of many days for a single woman given the unsettled situation. Travelling by train and river steamer, and hitchhiking some of the way by truck, she was happy to reach Kutsing in mid-west China (present day Qujing in eastern Yunnan province) and to find a room in the hostel of the Friends' Ambulance Unit (the Friends were a Quaker group that provided medical help to both Chinese people and foreigners in China).

As soon as she arrived at the hostel, Mother began to explore how she could get to Kunming, still many hours to the south. There were no trucks going to Kunming, where her fiancé, Norman Charter, waited for her, but she learned there was sometimes a train that went there. In those days there were no passenger cars on trains, so people sometimes travelled on top of the boxcars, often falling off and losing a limb or even their life. The Friends' Ambulance Unit were familiar with this scenario, because many of the injured were brought to their hospital for medical treatment.

The Yunnan Special

There seemed to be no other option than this "Yunnan Special," which reminded Mother of a cattle train in Canada. With fear and lots of prayer, she prepared to travel by rail—alone. The night before she was to leave, she went to an evening prayer meeting at the Quaker hostel. She was a bit late, so she sat near the door. A few minutes later, the door behind her opened. Without looking up from her hymnbook, she pulled up a chair beside her.

When she moved to share her hymnbook with the latecomer, she looked up into the eyes of her fiancé, Norman Charter! She hadn't seen him in four or five years. He had come that day by train from Kunming to Kutsing, on the odd chance that maybe his fiancée, my mother, might have gotten that far on her journey. Imagine their joy at finding each other in the evening prayer meeting! All her fears of the long journey alone the next day melted into thin air.

Early the next morning they went to the train station, thinking they'd get ahead of others in the lineup for a place on the train to Kunming. However, it was Chinese New Year and, as happens still, most of China was going home to celebrate with family. There were no seats. My parents waited on the platform well into the afternoon, when finally a loaded freight train arrived, crowded with people sitting and standing in every available space. Some were already riding on the top of the cars. With no other option, my mother and father climbed onto the top of the train. Norman hoisted his fiancée's boxes to the top and then, with ropes, he pulled Evelyn to the roof of the train as well.

And so, like good Canadian hobos riding the rods, they made themselves as comfortable as possible for the long night ahead, wrapping a tarp they had found in Evelyn's boxes around themselves. As they waited for the journey to start, Norman tried to unpack blankets from Evelyn's boxes to keep them warm. Unfortunately, they were awkwardly perched on the top of the train as it began to move, and Evelyn's coat slipped over the edge and into the dark night. Norman wanted so much to climb down and get the coat—but Evelyn wouldn't even think of it. She was taking no chances of losing him again.

I'm sure that on a fourteen-hour ride on top of a freight train, through the dark, cold winter night of midwestern China, Norman came up with ways to keep Evelyn warm and she found ways to keep him from falling off the train! They were married six months later in Kunming.

Adventure Is in My Genes

People ask me if I am naturally adventurous. I tell them I sometimes think I'm genetically wired for risky experiences. Or is it that adventure just seems to find me? Coping with impossible situations seems to be in my blood. When I read my mother's stories from World War II in China, I realize that I inherited a willingness to take risks from her. I know it isn't just love for adventure. My willingness to venture into danger depends on whether the situation aligns with one of the passions of my heart.

I am a woman with three passions, and I organize my life around them. When I have to make a decision, I go back to my passions and ask whether the decision I'm making is in line with them. When I wake up in the morning, I ask myself which passion will help me decide what I should do today. It's my way of using time well.

Passion Number One: Unreached People Groups

My number one passion is for the millions in our world who, through no fault of their own, have never heard about Jesus. I love the unreached people[10]* on our planet. This passion was nurtured in me by the stories of my parents and grandparents, who lived and worked in China. I was born in the city of Tali, the backpackers' haven of southwest China, Yunnan province. On October 1, 1949 the People's Republic of China was established by Mao Zedong. I was born one month later on November 1st. For the first two years of my life, my family was put under house arrest by the newly established communist regime.

After the revolution of 1949, my parents watched as the unbelievable happened right before their eyes. My father had grown up in China, so China was "home" to him. It was also the world's largest mission field. Then in 1949, nearly one quarter of the world's population came under communist rule. Speaking openly about Jesus in China suddenly became illegal. China became a hard place for international workers to live. My father had to stop climbing in the mountains of southwest China, where

---

10 People enthusiastic about missions speak about unreached or least-reached people, a group among whom there is no indigenous community of believing Christians with adequate numbers and resources to evangelize their own people without outside assistance. See the definition used by the Joshua Project at https://joshuaproject.net/unreached/1 (accessed May 20, 2020).

for years he had discovered tribal people who had never heard about Jesus. He discovered people like the Lisu, the Nosu, and the Mhong living deep in the forests, hidden from public view. These people groups* were his passion.

He wasn't a healthy man, but that didn't get in the way of his determination to take the Good News about Jesus to people living high in the mountains around Siangyun in southwest China. He was sometimes the first white person these mountain dwellers had ever seen. None of them had ever heard of Jesus. He passed to me his love for people who have never heard of Jesus, and they became my first passion. This passion was nurtured in my heart by my father, who grieved for his tribal friends long after we left China.

Passion Number Two: The Suffering Church

Every time my parents told me the story of the day our family was forced out of China, they cried. I was only sixteen months old in 1951 when Mao's communist regime gave thousands of missionaries one day's notice to leave China. We had been house prisoners almost from the day of my birth. Every day, my father would go to the authorities to ask if our family had been cleared to leave China. The authorities would tell us they were checking to make sure that we didn't have unsettled debts. Were there accusations by locals which could be used to extort money from us before we left?

After many months, the day finally arrived. Permission was granted, and we were given twenty-four hours to leave. My father's eyes always filled with tears as he told his children about that day. Only a handful of Chinese Christians had courage to gather around us to say goodbye. They didn't know that they were entering a period of unprecedented suffering under Mao.

I was a baby in my mother's arms when my parents and their three children walked to the outskirts of the city of Siangyun with just the clothes on their backs. My mother flagged down a truck loaded with oranges, and with me in her arms, she pulled another toddler, a seven-year-old, and her husband, who was almost an invalid, onto the pile of fruit. And we began to hitchhike across southern China—a journey to Hong Kong that would take several weeks, a journey that would eventually end in Canada.

My father died when I was twenty-three years old. I think he died prematurely of a broken heart, praying for persecuted Christians around the world. He would cry as he prayed for the believers he'd left behind in China. The seeds of a passion for the suffering church were already growing in my heart when I heard his stories from China.

Is it surprising that as a young woman I went to communist Europe to work with the suffering church? My heart was drawn to the secretive underground ministry to pastors and their wives. I had discovered a mission group who shared my passion for those who suffer because of their willingness to be known as followers of Jesus. In 1984, I joined an underground training program for pastors who lived behind the Iron Curtain.*

Passion Number Three: The Next Generation
I love the next generation—those who will lead God's church when people like me are dead. I wrote this book for them. I often run into young and middle-aged adults who heard my "missionary stories" when they were children. This book is part of the legacy I want to leave for the next generation.

He Told Us His Story

During the 1980s, I travelled back and forth across Romania by train, teaching women in the underground training program. The women loved to hear my stories of growing up with three brothers and three sisters in small-town western Canada, listening to my father tell his own stories of growing up in China. My students, most of them pastor's wives, had many questions about my unimaginably privileged life, living with total freedom to pass faith to the next generation. In the eighties in Romania, it was almost a crime to teach a child under twenty-one years of age about God. Tell me, how can you pass faith to the next generation if the government limits what you can teach even your own children about God?

Using the image of a relay race, the question the women most often asked was, "What was your parents' secret in passing faith to the next generation? What did they do that resulted in all seven of their children grabbing the baton and entering the race of faith?" The fact that all seven of us had followed hard after God was astounding to the pastors and their wives. It seemed unusual to them that not one of seven children had "dropped the baton." Maybe it really was as unusual in that time as it is today.

When they asked me how my parents had done this, I was never quite sure how to respond. My mother wasn't sure how to answer the question, either. She didn't want to take credit for something she hadn't done. But long after both parents died, I realized one day that I knew the answer. It was simple—my father had told us his story.

My father died forty-nine years ago. I can hardly remember his face, but I remember his stories! I'll admit, he was a very good storyteller—but the stories he told us were the kind that anyone can tell. Without us even realizing it, his stories answered three very simple yet strikingly profound questions. I discuss these questions with every young person I mentor: Who am I? Who is God? And what is my purpose in life?

Three Simple Questions

As my father told stories to us, we children listened, unconsciously finding in his stories the answers to those three questions. Many years later, I realize that as he told his stories, I was coming to understand who I am—that is, who God created me to be. Through his words, my father also passed along to us his understanding of who God is. His stories revealed to us the character of God. And, over time, they helped each one of his children to begin to formulate a response to the question of life purpose. Through his stories, we began to understand more fully why we had been born.

1) Who Am I?

For most of us, the question "Who am I?" is as good a starting place as any. We grow up trying to figure out who we are. Unfortunately, in North America we are socialized to believe that we are defined by what we have, what we do, or what other people think of us.[11] Our culture wants us to believe that these are the things that define who we are.

Wrong! That isn't the true self. My true identity is the person God intended me to be when he created me. It's a gift from God, not something I can achieve.[12] God has invited us into a life-long process of discovering who he created us to be. Those discoveries are an important part of the process we call discipleship. I'm passionate about helping the next generation begin to understand who God created them to be. I find myself returning, over and over, to my perpetually growing understanding of who God created me to be.

Picture my father with his seven children around him at bedtime, telling us stories about his childhood in China. He could tell us those stories over and over without them becoming boring. No stories brought more laughter from us than his first-person accounts of a very naughty little boy named Norman Charter who often disobeyed and then was punished by his parents.

My favourite was his story of misbehaving at bath time. The bathrobe of his younger brother, Cyril, got totally soaked. My father would chuckle and pretend

---

11   M. Basil Pennington, *True Self/False Self* (New York: Crossroad, 2000), p. 31.

12   David Benner, *The Gift of Being Yourself: The Sacred Call to Self-Discovery* (Downers Grove, IL: InterVarsity Press, 2004), p. 47.

to be ashamed as he told us how he brought the dripping bathrobe to his father, as though he were one of Joseph's brothers approaching father Jacob with the blood-soaked robe of many colours.

Playfully, he'd ask his father, playing the role of young Joseph, "Is this your son's robe?"

In our minds, the answer to a rhetorical question was forming: how could our daddy be such a rascal? How could he be sinful, and yet God had chosen him to be his child all the same? It was reassuring to us that although this man whom we loved and admired had been a naughty boy in childhood—a sinner—God loved him and chose him to be his child. God didn't choose him because he was perfect. Or because he'd never sinned. God chose my father because that's what God does. He chooses to love us in spite of our brokenness. That's why God chose Israel—not because of any goodness in Israel, not because Israel was bigger or better than another nation. He chose Israel just because he loved them and wanted to use these people he had chosen to accomplish his purposes in the world.

Pieces of the Puzzle: As I think about the question "Who am I?" I have to stop and acknowledge that God has created me mysteriously wonderful and quite different from anyone else. I bring different puzzle pieces to the picture which, when fit together, explain who I really am. The pieces don't make sense on their own, but when seen as parts of the whole, help me accept how important each piece is.

Chosen: For example, I wonder why, out of billions of people in this world, God chose *me*. Why did God call me to himself when I was seven?

I can remember the night I knew he had chosen *me*. That night, the tormenting prospect of life forever separated from him was lifted from my seven-year-old mind. Even at such a young age, I realized that Jesus had died for *me*. He loved *me*. I was his child—his chosen child. Waking up from a frightening dream of hell, I ran to my mother's bed, shook her sleeping body awake, and asked how I could become a child of God.

That night, I received the free gift of forgiveness. The next morning at breakfast, mother questioned me in front of my siblings about what had happened during the night. I remember having a childish sense that in receiving the free gift of salvation, God had also called me to do something very special for him. That's pretty hard to believe, because I was only seven years old. But I have returned over and over to the certainty of God's call that night—first a call to be his child, and then a call to serve him. God saved and called me—not because of anything good in me, but just because he loves me. God can do that! He is God—it's as simple as that!

Understanding the question "Who am I?" is a fundamental part of answering the third question, "What is my purpose in life?" When Joshua stood with Israel at the Jordan River, he explained why Israel had gotten to witness the amazing miracle of a dry crossing of the Jordan. He said, *"[God] did this so that all the peoples of the earth might know that the hand of the Lord is powerful… "* (Joshua 4:24).

I believe that I was "called" or "chosen" so that, in some tangible way, my life would be a tool God uses to bring the nations to himself. Perhaps that explains my passion for unreached people groups—people who have never heard about Jesus.

Woman: I'm glad I am a woman, but at times I've had a hard time reconciling God's creation of me as a woman with an unusual sense of God's calling on my life, a calling to serve the church. That calling hasn't always made sense, as I discovered growing up in the church and then with a new painfulness when I first arrived in Romania. Until recent years, the church wasn't fully open to acknowledging God's call on my life. However, looking back, I realize that being a woman was important to my accomplishing the purpose for which God created me. It's an important piece of who I am.

Single: I have wrestled with the puzzle piece of singleness more than any other aspect of who I am. Growing up, I always thought I would marry and have children. I am a people person. I like to nurture others. As the years passed, it became more and more clear that maybe I would never marry. The idea that God has chosen me became more and more important. To an extent, any pain encountered because I was single has been softened because I sense that it is an integral part of God's design. Could it be that I can only fulfill his purpose for my life if I am single?

It would be so much easier to embrace singleness if I didn't have to live with the desire for companionship. I like people, and Lord knows, I like men! I love community. What's more, I really wanted to marry! If I didn't have to deal with the natural, God-given desire for children, it might be easier to be single. My singleness is one of those aspects of myself that reminds me that although I don't understand God's sovereign choices, it's better for me to embrace them.

God, in his providence, is orchestrating the events of my life for good and for the fulfillment of his greater purpose. My life lived as a single woman is a pretty important piece of who I am. As I look back on the richness of the life God has allowed for me, I often say that I am "a completely fulfilled, continually hopeful woman." I feel great fulfillment in the life I've lived, but my hopefulness for marriage is always with me. It's a tension I live with.

2) Who Is God?

My father's stories of his naughtiness and repentance pointed to the grace and mercy of God. When I try to put into simple words my answer to the question "Who is God?" I find myself thinking about two concepts that frighten people who are intimidated by big, theological words: God's Sovereignty and his Providence.

Sovereignty and Providence: Sovereignty reminds me that God does whatever he wants to do. He is absolutely in charge of everything that happens in the world—and in my life. Providence speaks to the fact that God makes everything he does fit together with perfection. I sometimes think about who God created me to be, and wonder at his ability to take these pieces of the puzzle and make something that is exactly what he needed—and what he knew I needed—in order to accomplish his purpose for my life.

3) What Is My Purpose in Life?

God is sovereign. He can do whatever he wants to do. And in his providence, he makes it all fit together, using who he created me to be in fulfilling his big purpose for my life. Every time I tell my story, the pieces of the puzzle make more sense. Chosen. Woman. Single. Humanly speaking, I don't get it! But the older I become, the more I understand of his goodness, his faithfulness, and his wisdom in creating me the way he did and in using me to accomplish his purpose for my life.

Time to Reflect

1. Why are stories such a powerful way to communicate truth? Can you share an experience of the effectiveness of story in the life of someone you know?
2. Where can we go in the Bible to explore the importance of telling stories to the next generation?
3. As you think about taking the Good News to hard places, what role might storytelling have?

Going Deeper

I always feel sad when I read the Old Testament book of Judges. The story of God's people begins to fall apart after they reach the Promised Land. When Moses knew God wouldn't let him go into the Land of Promise, he turned leadership over to Joshua. Over and over, Moses told Joshua to be sure to remind God's people of how God had taken care of Israel during forty years in the desert, even though they complained and badmouthed him all the time. Joshua was so good at telling stories about God's miraculous care for Israel.

But when Joshua died, it was as though storytelling died with him. Scripture tells us that after Joshua and his whole generation died and were buried, another generation grew up that didn't know anything about God or all the things he had done for Israel. The people of Israel became more and more evil. They served the gods of their neighbours. They walked away entirely from the God of their parents who had rescued them from Egypt (Judges 2:10–11).

Someone dropped the storytelling baton! Passing stories to the next generation had been God's way of keeping faith alive. It's sad to watch how the faith of the fathers disappeared from sight when the storytelling stopped.

Many years earlier, Joshua had stood in Canaan, on the east side of the Jordan River. He'd looked across the river and seen a land more fruitful than he had hoped for and more beautiful than he had ever imagined. This was the fulfillment of an ancient promise to Father Abraham[13] that his descendants would live in this land. Israel was pretty tired of wandering in the wilderness, which they had been doing for forty years. Can you imagine how they felt, funeral after funeral, as they buried an entire generation that would never enter the Promised Land? Finally, they were ready to go into Canaan. All that now stood between Israel and the land that God had promised them was the Jordan River. But they had a problem. How do you move several million people across one of the major rivers in Palestine when the water level is at its seasonal peak?

Standing at the river's edge, watching its menacing speed, the people knew that below the rapid currents and swirling, muddy waters were hidden boulders and dangers. They found themselves between a rock and a hard place, that's for sure. But God, their Rock, was right there. He performed a miracle that sounded a lot like the stories their grandparents had told about Israel's Exodus from Egypt. In a *déjà vu* moment, God rolled back the waters of the Jordan River—just as he had done with the Red Sea. It was as though God was once again writing his signature in the impossible.

Scripture tells us that the moment the feet of the priests who carried the things Israel used in worship touched the river, the water further upstream simply stopped flowing! It just *"piled up in a heap"* (Joshua 3:16). The priests walked out to the

---

13   In Genesis 15:18, God promised Abram, *"To your descendants I give this land, from the river of Egypt to the great river, the Euphrates…."* The promise was confirmed to Abraham's son Isaac in Genesis 26:3, and then to Isaac's son Jacob in Genesis 28:13. It was referred to as the Promised Land because it was the land promised to Abraham (see Exodus 23:31).

middle of a bone-dry riverbed and waited for several million people to walk to the other side (verse 17). Breathtaking!

Can you imagine: several million people crossed the river that day, and they didn't even get wet feet! Then God told Joshua to choose twelve men, one from each tribe of Israel, to find a big stone in the middle of the riverbed. Boulders had been exposed by the miraculous "piling up" of the water. The men carried the boulders to the other side and set them down in the Promised Land. Those big stones were stacked in one enormous pile, an unmistakable marker at the very place where God had shown his power over the Jordan River.

What Do These Stones Mean?

Why the pile of stones? Those stones marked an important site. In the years that followed, people would see that pile of boulders—a memorial to God's power. Children would ask, "Hey Dad, hey Grandma—what do those stones mean?" God knew they'd ask because that's what kids do. His instruction was, *"One day your children will ask you, 'What do these stones mean?' Tell them your story!"* (Joshua 4:6b–7, my paraphrase). The pile of stones became a platform from which amazing stories of God's faithfulness were launched.

The memorial of stones cried out, "God did this! By his hand we crossed the raging Jordan on dry ground. By his power and faithfulness, we survived the impossible." The stories of that generation pointed to God. Those stones—and the stories the fathers told their children—were also a constant reminder of Israel's purpose in life. God told them there was only one reason why he had done to the Jordan River exactly what he had done to the Red Sea. He dried it up so that all the peoples of the earth would know how powerful he was (Joshua 4:23–24).

The people of Israel seemed tempted to think that God had chosen them from among many nations because of something inherently special in them. That wasn't the case at all! Moses didn't mince his words in reminding them that God hadn't chosen them because they were bigger or better than other people (Deuteronomy 7:7). In fact, they were the smallest group imaginable—insignificant! He reminded them that God had rescued them from slavery just because he loved them (verse 8) and because he was keeping promises made to their grandparents (verse 9).

Every time an Israelite man or woman told a child about crossing the Jordan River, the story pointed to who God is. It reminded them of the limitations every human feels in the face of impossible things. We feel very small when we find ourselves between a rock and a hard place—just because we are human! The story pointed to the purpose of God in choosing Israel as his beloved people, so that *"all the peoples of the earth might know that the hand of the Lord is powerful"* (Joshua 4:24). Ultimately, the nations of the earth are in God's sight when he steps into impossible situations. That's why he gets involved.

A Kind of Amnesia

The women are gathering again in the living room of Pastor Teo and his wife, Sanda. We haven't met for several months because travel in Romania is harsh during the winter. A request for a tourist visa at the border sounds rather ridiculous at this time of year. No tourist in her right mind would choose Romania as a wintertime destination!

Gatherings have also been postponed recently because leaders want to rethink who can be trusted to join the circle of women in this new program. Everyone is wondering if there is an informer in the group. How did the secret police learn about our meeting three months ago? Why did Pastor Teo get called to the secret police for questioning after we left town in the summer? The men are absolutely certain that every woman in the group can be trusted. But the pervading culture of distrust in Romanian society makes the women suspicious of each other. They seem cautious about sharing their personal thoughts and concerns in the group.

If family concerns and the pain of their present situation are leaked to the ears of the secret police, those tidbits of personal life might be used against them to intimidate and control. If they hear the secret police in an interrogation session say, "We just happen to know that ...," the pastor or his wife will know they have been busted.

All afternoon I feel the tension in the room as I illustrate the lesson, sharing openly from my own spiritual struggles and personal experiences. An old lady, dressed completely in funeral black, sits quietly all afternoon, eyes fixed on the floor, never lifting them to meet mine. I know she is living with pain, though she would never dare to express it openly. She misses her husband so much, but she can't talk about it. She has no safe place where she can unburden her heart, so she sits all day in silence, her sad eyes gazing on her folded hands.

As we come to the end of the day, I suggest we finish by praying in small groups for one another. Suddenly the women realize that praying together requires some vulnerable sharing of need. Fear rises in their eyes. Before we begin to share and pray, the woman in black raises a trembling hand. She wants to say something. With frightened eyes she glances awkwardly around the circle, looking courageously into her sisters' eyes. In a quiet voice she addresses the circle of women: "Sisters, we have a lot to learn about what Miriam is modelling for us every time she is with us. We feel closer to Miriam than we do to each other, though we've known Miriam for only a few months." Heads are nodding. "Why is that?" she asks.

There is silence as the women ponder her question. She doesn't wait for their response as she continues, "We feel closer to Miriam because she tells us her story!"

* * *

Thirty-five years later I am back in Romania (2019 and 2020), interviewing the same women to whom I told stories as part of my teaching during the dark days of communism. Now it is their turn to tell stories of God's faithfulness, this time without fear that a member of the group around the table is an informer or that their personal experiences might fall into the wrong hands. Their grown children or little grandchildren sometimes sit with us at the table, listening in wide-eyed wonder as parents and grandparents recount stories of "crossing the Red Sea on dry ground," this time with the secret police in determined pursuit.

With persistence, I ask questions that I hope will pull from these aging men and women stories of the good old (or bad old) days when God did the impossible. I realize that this is the first time some of their descendants have heard the stories I'm trying to capture for the book. Over and over, at the end of these conversations, I hear grown children say to their parents, "We love these stories! Why have we never heard them till now?"

I ask my former students the same question. One wise woman responds with unusual insight: "The communist era is an unhealed wound in our past. The December Revolution in 1989 happened and gave us a legitimate chance to forget the pain. We really don't want to tell our children about those painful parts of our history. It's easier to forget."

Another woman, old enough to remember what God did for his people during the communist years, reflects on what she calls "collective amnesia" in the church. She wonders if there is a general preference to forget.

In the post-Revolution era, the church tried to make up for decades of lost time. There was no time to think about the past—no time to tell stories. Christians were busy; the opportunities facing the church, with its new freedoms, consumed their time and energy. Stories were lost to future generations because by the time the church was settled into a new normal, many stories had been forgotten.

Claudio is the adult son of one of the pastors who loves to tell me stories of God's faithfulness during the communist years. Claudio wonders if believers have tried to deal with history as their teachers at school did. Right after the Revolution in 1989, Claudio's Romanian literature teacher showed the class how to get rid of the parts of history that he thought people should forget. Without apology, the teacher told his students which pages of their Romanian literature text to get rid of, holding up the book in front of them and ripping from the textbook every page on which their "inglorious leader," Ceausescu, was glorified. As though it were that easy to delete the painfulness of the past and rewrite history! I asked Claudio's father if that was how Christian parents have dealt with the stories of their suffering during the years of communist oppression—simply blotting it from the record. Have they forgotten how God uses story to pass faith to the next generation?

My mind returns to the generation that followed Joshua's death: a generation that seemed to know very little about what God had done for Israel at the Red Sea, at the Jordan River, and in reclaiming the Promised Land. Was it that parents didn't tell the stories, or was it that children didn't ask? Or was it both? Were they just caught up in the new delights of being in the Promised Land, too busy establishing themselves in the land of milk and honey?

As the story of Joshua closes (Judges 2:10–11), we read about a new generation growing up, knowing nothing about God or what he had done for Israel. Someone dropped the storytelling baton. The next generation *"did evil in the Lord's sight"* (verse 11), turning their back on the God of their fathers. Parents didn't tell their stories, and so missed an opportunity to point to the unsurpassed goodness of God. Were they ashamed to tell of their fathers' lack of faith in the face of impossible situations, even though God had already shown that there was no obstacle he couldn't overcome? Are Romanians still trying to understand who they are and who God is? Are they still trying to figure out what their purpose in life is?

Perhaps that's why it's so important for me to tell the stories you read in this book. Passing stories to the next generation is God's way of keeping faith alive. This might be one of my contributions to the rising generation.

Going Further: Recommended Reading

Benner, David. *The Gift of Being Yourself.* Downers Grove, IL: InterVarsity Press, 2015.

Enns, Peter. *Telling God's Story: A Parent's Guide to Teaching the Bible.* Charles City, VA: Olive Branch Books, 2011.

Doing Ministry in Hard Places: Ethical Issues

CHAPTER THREE

I Tell a Lie

The old train moans as it moves through the night toward Romania's western border with Hungary. I am looking forward to sleeping in my own bed in Vienna tonight. I fight sleep, knowing we will very soon arrive at the border. On my mind is a conversation earlier in the day with two pastors in the city we just left. They told me about the well-orchestrated plan of the Ceausescu government to undermine the church and bring about its ultimate destruction. They asked me to take this news to the Commission on Security and Cooperation in Europe, meeting these days at the Hofburg Palace in Vienna.[14] They want Western media to hear about the grievous human rights violations of the Ceausescu regime in Romania.

Tucked into the false bottom of my suitcase, along with my notes from their briefing, are the names of pastors who face relentless intimidation, threats, and abuse by the secret police, all of it written in coded language. I will take this incriminating information to the head of the Human Rights Commission, US Senator Hoyer, who is waiting in Vienna for the news I carry.

At 4:30 a.m., the train begins to slow and shudders to a stop at Curtici, the border crossing with Hungary. The atmosphere in the compartment is tense as everyone prepares for the unpredictable questions of the border police. I try not to think about the sensitive information I'm carrying.

---

14   For forty years, the Commission on Security and Cooperation in Europe has monitored how nations comply with the Helsinki Accords and contributed to security in the fifty-seven-nation region covered by the OSCE (Organization for the Security and Cooperation in Europe), promoting regional cooperation on human rights, democracy, the economy, the environment, and military matters. As a result of its work, "violations of Helsinki provisions were given full consideration in U.S. foreign policy" during the communist years, and it was assumed that "human rights violations" were "a legitimate subject for one country to raise with another." ("About the Commission on Security and Cooperation in Europe," https://www.csce.gov/about-commission-security-and-cooperation-europe, accessed September 2, 2020).

Glancing out the dirty windows, we see men in army greens waiting on the platform for the doors of the train to be unlocked. Soon we hear them enter the train and pound down the corridor to the compartment where we wait. We hear the barks of their drug-sniffing dogs. Without ceremony, an officer throws open the door of our compartment and barks the command, *"Paşapoarte!"*

I feel an evil presence has entered the compartment. The border official turns to me as soon as he sees the name on my passport. It is as though they have been waiting for me. To the exclusion of everyone else in the compartment, he barks at me in a single word the question, *"Documente?"*—"Do you have documents on you?"

The directness of his question catches me off guard. There is no time to compose an evasive response or to disarm the intensity of his attack by asking him a question in return. His question demands either a "Yes" or a "No."

Without hesitation, I respond with a simple but convincing "No!" I know that if the documents I carry are discovered in the search of my luggage, I will be taken off the train and held for interrogation. The consequences will be grave for all the pastors whose contact information I have hidden under the false bottom of my suitcase.

The immediacy of my response to his question seems to surprise him. He moves on to the others in the compartment, motioning to the soldier with him to search our luggage.

Confusion erupts as eight standing humans, one sniffing canine, and many bags and suitcases soon fill the floor of the very small compartment. Without digging deeply into my suitcase, the soldier opens a tube of toothpaste and squints into the opening. He obviously doesn't want to dig through the dirty underwear and damp towels he finds at the top of my suitcase! He grabs my teaching notebook and asks me, using mostly gestures, what it is. Pretending not to understand Romanian, I tell him it is a book I am writing, which has some truth in it.

Realizing they still have many more travellers to question and search, they move to the next compartment. An hour later they leave the train. It is an unsettling hour for me. I feel the guilt of telling an outright lie to the customs official. The weight of guilt feels heavier because Yvonne, my travelling companion, knows what is under the false bottom of my suitcase. She knows I lied! In briefing her for travel two weeks earlier, I told her that our practice is not to tell lies at border crossings or in any interactions with officials. There are better ways, I told her, of answering difficult questions.

Doing the Will of God

Back in Vienna, I wrestle with the dilemma of having concealed that part of the truth that would have hurt a brother in Christ. I ask myself if this time I have pushed not telling the truth for the sake of God's kingdom too far. It is little comfort to remember that there are, nevertheless, many Christian brothers and sisters alive and still serving God's church in Romania as a result of my quick decision.

One afternoon the guilt I have carried for weeks becomes too heavy to bear. I go to the basement of the old house where we have our office to speak with my boss, Bill. He listens quietly to my story. What had once been a strong sense of calling to the suffering church has begun to take on elements of shame. Perhaps I'm not suited for ministry in countries where the people of God suffer because they are willing to be known as followers of Jesus, where the government would disapprove if they knew what we were doing, where the rules for ministry look like rules of war, not rules of peace.

Bill's gentle response is first to remind me that God had witnessed and will forgive the lie I told at the border to protect his people. Turning to 1 John 1:9, he reads out loud to me, *"If we confess our sins, he is faithful and just and will forgive us our sins and purify us from all unrighteousness."* He reminds me, however, that the assurance of God's forgiveness is never a license to sin.

But in a sense, everything about ministry in a Creative Access Nation* like Romania requires a certain amount of deception: my explanation at borders that I work for a travel agency in Canada (which gets me into many countries just because of the tourist dollars I might bring in). Wearing old clothing on the streets so the secret police won't follow me to the homes of believers. Using a false name for myself, knowing that believers might be called to the authorities for interrogation after I leave town, fearing they might, inadvertently, divulge my real name.

Carefully, we process the promise in 1 John 1:9. We pray together, and I entrust my anxious spirit to the Judge of all the earth, knowing that he will do what is right (Genesis 18:25).

Then, almost as if Bill had prepared for my coming, he opens to Hebrews chapter 11, turning immediately to where Rahab the prostitute's name is found. Rahab told a lie, perhaps not even a necessary lie, to protect God's people (Hebrews 11:31). She is named with honour among the heroes of our faith, even given a place in the direct birth line of Christ (Matthew 1:5). The reminder is comforting to me.

I leave Bill's office to reflect once again on the apologetic I so carefully developed before I moved to Europe (see next section) for ministry in a hard place. My well-developed ethical framework is comforting in a new way. Christ said, *"… go and make disciples of all nations… And surely I am with you always, to the very end of the age"* (Matthew 28:19–20). I know that in obeying that command, I am doing the will of God. I go home to think again about the ethics of doing ministry in hard places.

Time to Reflect

1. What is the missional dilemma this story raises? Is it an issue those who take the Good News to hard places will deal with today?
2. What do you already know about the ethical issues involved in doing ministry in contexts where the government would disapprove if they knew what you were doing?
3. Where might you go to explore the issue more deeply? Biblical scholars, historians and theologians through the centuries, and missiologists (more recently) have debated the ethical issues of doing ministry in contexts sometimes called Creative Access Nations. The next section looks at the issue through the lenses of theology, history, and the experience of the church today.

Going Deeper

As a senior in high school, I was captivated by a modern-day missionary story called *God's Smuggler*[15] in which a Dutch believer, known simply as "Brother Andrew," engaged in covert, cloak-and-dagger ministry behind the Iron Curtain. The book fascinated young people in my generation, and played a significant role in the call of many to ministry with the persecuted church.

My early years in China gave me a little exposure to the impact a militant communist regime could have on the church. As a young person, I often discussed with my father the question of whether there are limits to a king's power over those he rules. He had invested many years in the church in China. In the early 1950s, he watched as Chinese believers courageously refused to give in to the new regime's harsh demands. He and his Chinese believing friends would have agreed with the

---

15 First published in 1967, the book had sold over ten million copies in thirty-five languages by 2002. Its publication abruptly ended Brother Andrew's access to all the countries for which he was passionate. See "Andrew van der Bijl," *Wikipedia* (https://en.wikipedia.org/wiki/Andrew_van_der_Bijl, accessed September 2, 2020); John and Elizabeth Sherrill and Open Doors International, *God's Smuggler* (Bloomington, MN: Chosen Books, 1967, 2001, 2015).

Reformers of the sixteenth century—men like John Calvin—that there are limits to a government's authority over its people.[16]

In 1984, I joined a group of international workers from Vienna who were bringing biblical education to pastors in communist Eastern Europe. We knew that this calling would lead to activities that went against established government policies in these countries. As I prepared to join the ministry (see Appendix), I spoke in churches in Canada, raising financial and prayer support for the ministry to which God was calling me.

One day a Christian attorney in a church approached me after I spoke. "How can you think about inviting Christians to support a ministry in countries where governments will view it as illegal?" he asked. "Have you forgotten that believers, if discovered to be cooperating with the Western church, might face a prison sentence or even death?" He cautioned me to be very sure that the church in Romania understood the danger attached to their invitation. I explained that pastors valued the training so much they were willing to accept the risks.

He wasn't the only one asking such questions. I realized I needed to develop a clear and biblical answer to the question, "Should the church in the West be involved in taking the Good News to any country where, if the government of that country knew what we were doing, it would not approve?" I called my answer "The Ethics of Smuggling," and presented it in churches and Christian colleges all over North America. It is an important issue for the next generation of international workers who will go to hard places.[17]

The Goal of Christian Ethics
Stated very simply, I believe the goal of Christian ethics is to do the will of God. I also believe that the principles of conduct that enable Christians to do the will of God are revealed in Scripture, and when seen as a system, they meet the requirements of

---

16 John Calvin, in his *Institutes of the Christian Religion*, speaks about the relationship between church and state. He believes that "God has established an order by which human beings ought to organize their civic lives so that piety (true faith) can flourish" (Book 4, Chapter 20, Parts 1–5: "Civil Religion," *John Calvin for Everyone* [http://www.johncalvinforeveryone.org/chapter-20-parts-1-5.html, accessed September 2, 2020]).

17 Twenty years ago, I was invited to give a lecture on this topic at a Christian university in Canada. University leaders refused to advertise my lecture called "The Ethics of Smuggling," citing their inability to think of "smuggling" as something "ethical." They were afraid of the negative repercussions that might result. The juxtaposition raised issues in the minds of university leaders, issues they had never had to deal with in the free West. I was asked to "soften" the title of my lecture by removing references to smuggling, because the word implies that the law is broken and is often associated with narcotics and illegal immigration.

an ethical order for all people for all time (Romans 14:18). The goal of Christian ethics is to do the will of God. The principles of conduct that enable Christians to do the will of God are revealed in Scripture.

Navigating this ethical system implies that we are dealing with a dilemma. Ethics, as a system of thought, calls on Christians to wrestle with controversy. As I grappled with the attorney's question, it was helpful to keep this stated

> The goal of Christian ethics is to do the will of God. The principles of conduct that enable Christians to do the will of God are revealed in Scripture.

purpose of Christian ethics in mind. I knew I needed to develop an ethical framework for a missional church in countries where the gospel is suppressed and even perceived as illegal. Churches doing ministry in such countries also need this framework.

God's Call

My rationale and ethical thinking were rooted in a personal sense of God's call to serve him in "closed" countries, which we sometimes refer to as "Limited Access Nations"* (LANs) or "Creative Access Nations" (CANs). I knew God had created me to serve him in places where the church is persecuted. My birth in southern China just before the exodus of thousands of missionaries in the early 1950s had a profound impact on my sense of destiny.

In 1983, God called me to leave a comfortable church position and join a project in Romania. Because of the communist regime that was in power, Romania was hostile to most Westerners—even to people in business, but especially to anyone who self-identified as a "missionary." We met in secret with believers who risked their lives every time they met with us. Meetings were sometimes cancelled because news of our meeting had been leaked to the secret police by informers within our group. Usually we would arrive in a train station, but we wouldn't be met by a host and taken directly to the home where the meeting would happen. Rather, we would look into the crowd on the station platform for a contact with whom we had pre-arranged a signal. For several years the signal we looked for was a man holding a small child, in whose hand was a yellow rubber duck. That person would lead us by a circuitous route to the secret gathering that night. We were usually disguised as peasants so the station police wouldn't know Westerners had arrived in town.

My call to this kind of ministry in 1983 came with an Old Testament promise that God was sending an angel ahead of me to guard me along the way and to bring me to the place he had prepared for me (Exodus 23:20, 27). These verses also said he would send his terror ahead of me and even throw into confusion every nation I encountered. I couldn't ignore his promise that even my enemies would turn their backs and run.

Every trip into Romania was accompanied by miracles as border guards opened our suitcases, looking for things they called "illegal." They were looking for Bibles, drugs, and weapons, in that order of priority. If Bibles or Christian literature were found in our bags, we would be denied entry. The words *persona non grata*[18] would be stamped in our passport. If that happened, we were turned away at the border, and not told how long we'd be banned from re-entry.

For these reasons, most ministries left the smuggling of Bibles and literature to organizations like Brother Andrew's mission group "Open Doors." There were plenty of young people on summer mission trips who were willing to take the risks involved in Bible smuggling. These young people were seen as more "expendable" than those of us who were full-time teachers in the underground Bible school program. Besides, groups like Open Doors had cleverly reconstructed vehicles with compartments where Bibles and literature could be concealed and successfully transported across communist borders. They would be delivered under cover of darkness to believers at the other end. Nevertheless, some people still accused us teachers of unethical ministry by virtue of the fact that deliveries were made on our behalf. Whether we liked it or not, we were involved with Bible smuggling!

The Biblical Mandate
"What about Romans 13?" the attorney in Canada pestered me. He read the first two verses to me:

> It is important that all of us submit to the authorities who have charge over us because God establishes all authority in heaven and on the earth. Therefore, a person who rebels against authority rebels against the order He established, and people like that can expect to face certain judgment.
> —Romans 13:1–2, VOICE (emphasis in original)

How was I supposed to respond to such words? My calling was to teach the Word of God. The geography had been confirmed to me: I was supposed to work in Eastern and Central Europe. But how could I teach the Word of God in a setting

---

18   The phrase literally means "an unwelcome person." It is a legal term used in diplomatic circles that indicates a foreign person who can no longer enter or remain in a country.

where Bible study is considered an anti-state activity and gatherings of more than three or four persons are illegal?[19]

I'd heard about believers in Romania who spent time in prison for transporting Christian books. Contact between citizens and Westerners was not permitted for two reasons: to keep Westerners from observing the truth about life in Romania,[20] and to ensure citizens never learned from travellers the extent of oppression by their government.

Three Witnesses

As I developed my plan to be involved with ministries in countries closed to the Good News, I imagined myself defending my rationale before a court of law. I brought three witnesses with me to the witness box: the witness of Scripture, the witness of church history, and the witness of the church in hard places today.

The Witness of Scripture: There are three things we need to understand from Scripture.

1. *We have permission to carry the gospel into enemy territory*

In both Acts 1:8 and Matthew 28:19–20, Christ's commission to move forward with the gospel in spite of enemies occupying parts of God's world is clear. Divine authority isn't limited by borders. That even includes countries ruled by evil dictators who defy the eternal King.

The best analogy I can offer for spreading the gospel is a state of war. The church has always been involved in a battle with evil (John 8:44; 2 Corinthians 4:4; 2 Corinthians 10:3–5, Ephesians 2:2; Ephesians 6:12; 1 Peter 5:8–10). Rules for wartime are quite different from rules in times of peace. For example, during World War II, the Allies did not ask permission or check out the local customs office before crossing enemy lines. Visitors to Romania in the 1980s often commented as they crossed into the country that they knew immediately they had moved into enemy territory. The sense of oppression and evil around them was palpable.

---

19 During the most oppressive years under President Nicolae Ceausescu in Romania (1980–1989), all gatherings of more than three or four were considered illegal because of the president's fear of internal uprisings among the populace. In the minds of the authorities, what better place for dissidents to plan a revolt than in a religious gathering?

20 The ministry I was a part of operated in Romania, Bulgaria, Czechoslovakia, Hungary, Poland, East Germany, and Russia. Most of this chapter refers to Romania, which at that time was believed to be the most militantly communist and the most brutal of these regimes in its treatment of believers. Though I worked in many of the other countries, most of the stories in this book took place in Romania. See Appendix.

My childhood hero, Brother Andrew, was such a passionate Christian, willing to engage in what some viewed as radical actions that violated government laws.[21] Brother Andrew took very seriously Christ's command to spread the gospel throughout the world, reclaiming every part of it for God (Matthew 28:19–20). When he was asked about his view on political borders, Brother Andrew explained it this way:

> You see, I don't believe that our Lord is willing for his Word and witness to be kept out of any country by guarded boundaries or government decrees. That would be contrary to both the spirit and letter of his commission to us to make disciples of all nations. In fact, doesn't it make better sense to concentrate efforts on those very spots that are most resistant to the gospel, most dominated by the devil's power?[22]

2. We need to understand what kinds of governments we should submit to

Scripture talks about the relationship between the believer, who belongs to the eternal kingdom of God, and the secular authority of an earthly government. Christians are told to obey authorities who uphold justice and suppress evil (1 Peter 2:13–17). At times, those qualities are pretty hard to quantify.

In communist Europe in the 1980s, and in countries today where Islamic regimes are in control, the lack of those qualities in government is obvious. Many governments, ruled by militant atheist* or Islamic rulers, reward evil and suppress what is good. In Romania during the eighties, the *"salt of the earth"* (Matthew 5:13) were under attack. Romans 13 and I Peter 2 teach that we are to submit to governments *because* they uphold justice, *because* they are God's instrument to carry out justice. That didn't describe the government of communist Romania.

3. God sometimes honours people because they disobey an earthly government

When I got to this point in my defense, the lawyer warned me that I was now on very thin ice, but I insisted that the Scriptures are filled with examples. When God's people, the Israelites, were slaves in Egypt, multiplying despite the ruthless treatment of their oppressors, the king of Egypt told Hebrew midwives to kill at

---

21   Some might compare Brother Andrew's views with Christian Libertarianism. Not to be confused with anarchism, libertarianism is a philosophy that combines liberty (the freedom to live your life in any peaceful way you choose), responsibility (the prohibition against the use of force against others, except in defense), and tolerance (honouring and respecting the peaceful choices of others). For a fuller explanation of libertarianism, see the website of the American Libertarian Party (https://www.lp.org/the-libertarian-party/, accessed September 2, 2020). It is the third largest political party in the United States, continuing to grow today.

22   Brother Andrew, *The Ethics of Smuggling* (Wheaton, IL: Tyndale House Publishers, 1974), p. 29.

birth any Hebrew boy that was born. This was his attempt to slow down the birth rate of the oppressed people over whom he ruled. When the king asked the Hebrew midwives why they were letting these boys live, they lied, saying that Hebrew women, unlike Egyptian women, gave birth even before the arrival of the midwives, and thus they had no opportunity to kill the babies. Exodus 1:21 says that *"because the midwives feared God, he gave them families of their own."* These women were honoured by God for their willingness to ignore the decree of an earthly king that threatened the future of God's people.

Rahab the prostitute hid the Hebrew spies and deliberately deceived her own rulers. She had in view another kingdom: the Kingdom of God. Her courageous faith in welcoming the spies and then lying to protect them earned her a place in the very birth line of Christ and in the hall of fame in Hebrews 11 (see verse 31 and Matthew 1:5).

1 Samuel 16 is a difficult passage that Western believers struggle to understand in addressing these questions. It is a good example of how sometimes God honours people who courageously stand against earthly rulers. While Saul was still king of Israel, failing badly at every turn, God told the prophet Samuel to anoint another dynasty[23] to take Saul's place. Samuel, who was deathly afraid of King Saul, was concerned about his reaction if he saw Samuel anoint someone else—afraid that Saul might even kill him.

In essence, God's instruction to Samuel, who was shaking in his boots, was, *"Don't tell them what you have come to do. Tell them you have come to sacrifice to the Lord"* (1 Samuel 16:2, my paraphrase). God himself told Samuel to stand against existing authority and conceal the truth—to hide his real mission from the king. As the age-long battle between good and evil raged, God authorized the prophet not to express the whole truth. According to God, Saul had no right to know the real purpose of Samuel's mission to Jesse, and Samuel was not obligated to share it with him.[24]

Deliberate concealment was an integral part of the strategy that enabled hundreds of Western missionaries to work in communist Europe in the 1980s. Believers in Romania didn't know our real names, lest under pressure during interrogation they would inadvertently disclose our identities. Each traveller had an authentic alias which helped us get visas. I worked for a travel agent in Calgary, Alberta, as a scout, looking for destinations for adventurous tourists. We often put on Romanian clothing once we crossed the border so as not to be immediately spotted as Westerners. In training Western travellers for a journey, we told them that our practice was

---

23 The great purpose of God was to maintain the line from which the Messiah would be born.

24 Brother Andrew, *The Ethics of Smuggling*, p. 42.

to not tell lies. We would answer direct questions from customs officials by asking a direct question in return. It disarmed the official. But the fact remained, everything we did involved concealment.

In the days of the early church, Peter and John, standing before the Jewish rulers, were commanded not to speak or teach in the name of Jesus. These men of God were pretty dissatisfied with that order and replied, *"You are the judges here, so we'll leave it up to you to judge whether it is right in the sight of God to obey your commands or God's.* But one thing we can tell you: *we cannot possibly restrain ourselves from speaking about what we have seen and heard* with our own eyes and ears" (Acts 4:17–21, VOICE, emphasis in original).

Again, Peter and other apostles were arrested and imprisoned for preaching and healing without a license. Does God condemn Peter for breaking the law? No, God comes to the defence of the accused, sending an angel to open prison doors for them—and then sending them back to the temple to preach the gospel, breaking the law again. When asked by the council why he had deliberately broken the law by teaching in Jesus' name, Peter replies, *"If we have to choose between obedience to God and obedience to any human authority, then we must obey God"* (Acts 5: 29, VOICE).

The Apostle Paul landed in prison over and over because he refused to obey the local government.[25] These were a few of many examples from Scripture that I brought to the witness stand to justify doing mission in nations where the government is hostile to Christianity.

The Witness of Church History: In every century there are examples of men and women of God who refused to obey human authority in order to further the mission of God in the world. They, too, are my heroes in faith. The church in this millennium owes a big debt to them for their courage. Jesus said, *"Everyone will hate you because of me"* (Luke 21:17). He warned them that they would have to testify before kings and governors because of Christ's name (Luke 21:12). According to tradition, all of the apostles except one died as martyrs during the first century A.D.[26] Each was martyred because of his refusal to bow to earthly government.

In the sixteenth century, Martin Luther split Europe because he stood up to governments, challenging the power of the pope and declaring the Bible to be the

---

25 Paul teaches, however, that Christians are to obey the law, provided the laws don't contradict the law of God. For example, we must never refuse to pay taxes: *"This is also why you pay taxes, for the authorities are God's servants, who give their full time to governing. Give to everyone what you owe them: If you owe taxes, pay taxes; if revenue, then revenue; if respect, then respect..."* (Romans 13:6). Jesus told his disciples to *"give back to Caesar what is Caesar's, and to God what is God's"* (Luke 20:25).

26 Only John, the writer of the Gospel of John and the book of Revelation, died a natural death.

only infallible authority. His courage to stand against the government and Church changed the course of Western civilization and made possible the translation of the Bible into the language of the people.

William Tyndale, an Oxford scholar and translator of the Bible from the original Greek and Hebrew to English, hid from the authorities for years. During those years, he printed thousands of copies of his translation and smuggled them into England. His translation spread quickly through the land. For decades, Bible readers in England were driven underground, facing death by burning just for owning a Bible in English. For more than a century, they waited for the King James Version of the Bible, which was based primarily on Tyndale's work.

Tyndale died as a heretic. He spent his last sixteen months in prison before he was executed by strangulation and burning, crying loudly so the crowd around him could hear his prayer, "God, open the eyes of the King of England." We have the English Bible today because of Tyndale's willingness to stand firmly against the established government and Church authorities.

The Witness of the Church in Hard Places Today: I found another witness which I brought with me as I tried to give an ethical answer to the lawyer's question. This time my witness was the church today in countries where it is under attack. For instance, if men and women hadn't had the courage to defy governments, the church in Eastern Europe might have quickly faced extinction during the communist era. Instead, I believe that the church survived and flourished *because* believers resisted evil governments and trusted themselves to God.

In today's world, atheistic, Islamic, or militaristic governments may tolerate Christianity but consider it to be opposed to the state. In many countries, it is often in the underground church, which is considered illegal, where one finds the real life of faith. That life seems to flow from conviction, holding tightly to the words of Jesus: *"...unless a grain of wheat is planted in the ground and dies, it remains a solitary seed. But when it is planted, it produces in death a great harvest"* (John 12:24, VOICE).

Believers in countries where Christians are hated quote the words of Tertullian, a second-century Christian theologian: "The blood of martyrs is the seed of the church." Through history, attempts by governments to wipe out the church have not only failed, but in a paradoxical way have led to its growth. Just as grass grows thicker and greener the more often it is mowed, so the church flourishes where governments try to eliminate it. A Romanian pastor in the mid 1980s who

> It is often in the underground church, which is considered illegal, where one finds the real life of faith.

studied in the underground training program said that Christianity is like a nail—the harder the government hits it, the deeper it goes! The promise of Jesus, *"… I will build My church. The church will reign triumphant even at the gates of hell"* (Matthew 16:18, VOICE), always rang in my ears while I travelled.

Open Doors, the organization that Brother Andrew began many years ago to bring Bibles, Christian literature, and humanitarian relief to the suffering church, is always updating its list of the fifty most oppressive countries, with governments that deny Christ and persecute Christians. Here are five examples from the 2020 World Watch list of places where the church continues to take a stand against governments:

- North Korea: Christians, if discovered, are sent to labour camps or killed on the spot.
- Afghanistan: There is no organized church; those who follow Jesus must do so in secret.
- Somalia: Most believers have to keep their faith completely secret as the consequence of being found out is most often death.
- Libya: Most believers have to keep their faith completely secret as the consequence of being found out is most likely death.
- Pakistan: Christian churches more active in outreach and youth work face strong persecution. The country's anti-blasphemy laws are disproportionately applied against the Christian minority.[27]

Today, more than 260 million Christians around the world face imprisonment, loss of home and assets, physical torture, beatings, rape, and even death as a result of their faith. To suggest that in order to live ethically a believer (whether inside the country or operating from outside) has to submit to the demands of governments that deny Christ makes a mockery of the lives of believers living in countries hostile to the gospel today. They live with courage and determination to do the will of God rather than to enable the rule of "another king." So, if living ethically as a Christian is about doing the will of God,

> To suggest that in order to live ethically a believer (whether inside the country or operating from outside) has to submit to the demands of governments that deny Christ makes a mockery of the lives of believers living in countries hostile to the gospel today.

---

27 "2020 World Watchlist," *Open Doors: Serving Persecuted Christians Worldwide* (http://www.open-doorsca.org/free-wwl-guide/, accessed September 2, 2020).

it is difficult to suggest that courageous and suffering believers in these countries are not living ethically.

With these arguments, I tried to answer my friend's question about taking the Good News to countries that have laws against doing so. He smiled and thanked me. Even if my answer didn't satisfy him, I held tightly to Peter's reply to the high priest and Jewish rulers: *"If we have to choose between obedience to God and obedience to any human authority, then we must obey God"* (Acts 5:29, VOICE).

The Ethics of Smuggling: Good News, Bibles, and Condoms

I ran into a troubling dilemma soon after I started travelling in Romania. My dilemma demanded an ethical answer, but it wasn't as easily resolved as issues involving smuggling Bibles or doing Christian ministry. The church in Canada came to accept the development of an underground training program for pastors and their wives as a "gospel ministry." They accepted the accompanying strategy we developed: Westerners travelling regularly into Romania, creating a full-study curriculum, and smuggling study materials into the country. However, the dilemma I now faced wasn't so easily resolved.

In one of my women's classes during the early eighties, the women confided in me a very personal problem. It had to do with marriage and childbearing in this country where family planning was strictly forbidden by the state.

One of Ceausescu's schemes for building socialism was to increase Romania's population from 23 million to 30 million by the year 2000. In 1966, he began his campaign with a decree that virtually made pregnancy a state policy: "The fetus is the property of the entire society. Anyone who avoids having children is a deserter who abandons the laws of national continuity."[28] All forms of contraception were declared illegal. Romania's birthrate nearly doubled at first, but poor nutrition and inadequate prenatal care endangered many pregnant women. Romania's infant mortality rate soared to eighty-three deaths in every one thousand births. About one in ten babies was born underweight. Newborns weighing 1500 grams (3 pounds, 5 ounces) or less were classified as miscarriages and refused treatment.[29]

The result of such evil decrees? In one group of women, I learned that some of them had lived with sexual abstinence for a long time—for years, some admitted. Some already had large families and were struggling to feed the children they had.

---

28 Karen Breslau, "Overplanned Parenthood: Ceausescu's Cruel Law." *Newsweek,* Jan. 22, 1990, p. 35.

29 Ibid.

They were afraid of getting pregnant because childbirth was a frightening prospect. If they couldn't pay the bribes asked by some doctors, they wouldn't be assured of a safe delivery. Hospital conditions were abysmal. Women got infections during childbirth that would plague them the rest of their lives. Food was always scarce, and milk and formula were rarities, so if a woman couldn't nurse her baby, the child's health was in jeopardy. Women often stood for eight hours in lines to obtain the most basic rations of food for families already close to starvation. The fear of conceiving another child was so frightening that many couples chose to live for years with sexual abstinence.

Discussions of birth control didn't excite my students. They told me that "natural" methods (checking fertility by taking your temperature and monitoring body fluids) weren't reliable, often resulting in another hungry mouth to feed, and all forms of contraception were banned by Ceausescu.[30] Among non-Christians, abortion was a widespread birth-control measure of last resort.[31] For Christians, it wasn't an option.

As our discussion deepened, the dilemma I perceived was that married couples who wanted to fully engage with each other had been abstaining from having sex. Believers confessed that sometimes the longing for sexual expression opened them to temptations to live in ways that they knew did not honour God.

The situation introduced me to an ethical dilemma I had never encountered before in ministry. I could contribute to the strength of the marriages of church leaders by providing a birth control solution—but it would require more "smuggling." In addition to students using "natural methods" of birth control, we could bring a form of contraception that would allow couples to build back into their marriages a form of sexual expression that would honour God and strengthen their marriages without conceiving another child.

We international workers started discussing our tendency to compartmentalize ministry into "spiritual" and "humanitarian" expressions of support. We could justify smuggling Bibles, but condoms? Scriptures like *"If anyone, then, knows the good they ought to do and doesn't do it, it is sin for them"* (James 4:17) were helpful. If the goal of my Christian ethics was to do the will of God, and I had the potential

---

30 Ceausescu made mockery of family planning. Sex education was forbidden. Books on human sexuality and reproduction were classified as "state secrets," to be used only as medical textbooks. With contraception banned, Romanians had to smuggle condoms and birth-control pills into the country (ibid.).

31 Ibid.

to contribute to a solution that nurtured the vitality of the marriage relationship between a pastor and his wife, shouldn't I get involved?

For several years during the final years of communism in Romania, every time I made a trip to Romania, in addition to a suitcase loaded with hard-to-get medications for someone, car parts for the aging car of a pastor, or sweets for the children, there would also be a large paper bag filled with fruit at my feet in the train compartment. Romanian border guards never questioned a Western traveller bringing a good supply of fruit to their country. They knew there was little fruit in the markets since most Romanian fruits and vegetables were exported to the West—another of Ceausescu's attempts to pay off the national debt while citizens starved. What border guards failed to discover was that beneath the apples, oranges, and bananas in the paper bag were hundreds of condoms for pastors in their country.[32]

I would arrive the next evening in the home of a Romanian leader, who, after a warm welcome and hug, would raise his eyebrows in a wordless question that asked, "Were you able to bring them?" A sheepish grin would cross his face as he exchanged knowing glances with his wife.

Going Further: Recommended Reading

Ripken, Nik. *The Insanity of God: A True Story of Faith Resurrected.* Nashville, TN: B&H Books, 2013.

Ripken, Nik. *The Insanity of Obedience: Walking with Jesus in Tough Places.* Nashville, TN: B&H Books, 2014.

---

32 Had they discovered the condoms, in the interest of concealing the whole truth, I would have raised eyes, brimming with innocence, to meet theirs and exclaimed, as any Western tourist might, "Well, I *am* in your country for two weeks!" My condom smuggling was never discovered at the border. What made this holistic ministry even more amusing was my trip to the pharmacy in Vienna before each trip, filling my little shopping basket with hundreds of condoms while onlookers (Viennese men are unabashedly snoopy) tried not to let me see their sideways glances of wonderment at a woman purchasing condoms of every sort, in large numbers, without apology.

Radical Identification:
Becoming Like Those We Serve

CHAPTER FOUR

"Becoming Like"

...let us in everything that is not sinful become like the Chinese that by all means we may save some.

—J. Hudson Taylor (quoting from 1 Corinthians 9:22)

Growing up, a favourite picture of my mother and father showed them in warm, padded jackets, the kind worn by uneducated country folk in China. I liked that picture, but I always thought my parents looked rather stiff and uncomfortable in their Chinese clothes. Did they enjoy dressing that way? Why did they do it?

One day my father explained to me that they wore Chinese clothes because of the example of Hudson Taylor (1832–1905), a missionary whom they really admired. Hudson Taylor started the China Inland Mission, the group with which my parents served in China. Very soon after arriving in China in 1854, Hudson Taylor made a pretty radical decision, considering the era he lived in. He decided to live as much like a Chinese man as he could so that nothing he did or wore would keep Chinese people from seeking after Jesus.

He didn't want the way he lived to raise curiosity in his Chinese friends about European culture. He really wanted them to be curious about Jesus. He was afraid that it might not happen if he looked like the proper English gentleman he really was. So, he moved right into a Chinese neighbourhood. He ate Chinese food. He tried to dress like the Chinese. He bought clothes that any Chinese schoolteacher would wear: thick calico socks, satin shoes with flat bottoms and curled-up toes (that squeezed his feet unmercifully), trousers that were two feet too wide around the waist and had to be folded in front and held in place with a belt. The billowy legs of his pants fell to just below the knee, and he tucked them into his socks. A white jacket with wide sleeves was covered with a silky gown with sleeves that reached twelve inches beyond his fingertips. He shaved his head, leaving only a little patch in the back. That tuft of hair eventually grew long enough to make into a pigtail, just like that of Chinese scholars he knew.

Hudson Taylor got lots of criticism from other Europeans who worked in China. And the Chinese didn't treat him with the same respect they gave to other Europeans. But very quickly he realized that the Chinese began to think of him as "just another one of us." Nobody was impressed by his European clothes or the fancy furniture in his home, things that shouted "British" when people dropped in to visit. His lifestyle meant that when a Chinese man came to see him, the man was sincerely interested in hearing about Jesus. The visitor wasn't dropping by just to see how this "black devil"[33] really lived. A beautiful bond of trust began to develop between Chinese people and this man. In missiological terms we say that Hudson Taylor tried to identify with the people he wanted to reach—he tried to live in a radically "incarnational" way.

Time to Reflect

1. What missional issue does the story of Hudson Taylor raise in your mind as you think about taking the Good News to a hard place today?
2. What do you already know about this issue? Have you had any experience with it?
3. Where can you go to explore the issue more deeply? Theologians through the centuries and international workers since the days of Hudson Taylor have wrestled to find ways to identify with the people to whom God sent them, believing it will lead to more effective ministry. In the next section we will look at the issue through the lenses of the life of Jesus, mission history, and my own experience in Romania.

Going Deeper

When I began to work in Romania, I remembered the story of Hudson Taylor. The picture of my mother and father dressed in padded Chinese jackets was lodged in my mind when I thought about working with the underground church in communist Romania, meeting with believers who risked their lives to welcome us into their homes.

When reading mission history, I noticed another helpful insight from the story of Hudson Taylor. He noticed that by wearing Chinese clothes he had far less trouble

---

33 When he first arrived in China, everywhere Hudson Taylor went he was referred to as a "black devil" because of the black, very "European" overcoat he wore.

with people who wanted to rob him. If he dressed as a European, people spotted him immediately in a crowd and targeted him as a potentially lucrative person to rob. If he wanted to pass unnoticed through a crowd, not causing a stir, he could do so if he was dressed like a Chinese man. No one picked him out as a foreigner. Life was a whole lot simpler when he tried to blend in and live like the people around him.

Becoming Like the Romanians

When I began to travel in Romania, I quickly realized we needed to figure out how to ride trains and walk in the streets without alerting the secret police that foreigners were in town. We didn't want to stand out as tourists in a crowd, especially in cities where it was against the law for foreigners to visit. In every train station there were plainclothes secret police who stood on the platform, studying the faces of everyone who left the trains. They were determined to keep foreign travellers from connecting with local citizens, especially despised followers of Jesus. We knew that if we appeared wearing trendy Western clothes and looking like real tourists, the secret police would follow us from the minute we left the train. Unfortunately, we might be the ones to lead them unintentionally to the home of the believers where we met.

In order to leave the train without being noticed and followed, we knew we couldn't dress like the Western tourists we'd declared ourselves to be at the border.[34]

Back home in Vienna, we spent hours in second hand stores buying unfashionable clothes: a dowdy old coat, well-worn shoes or boots, a cheaply made purse, a battered old suitcase, and usually a big wool scarf that we affectionately called our *babushka*,[35] a covering that we pulled up onto our heads before we left the train. The only part of ourself that people could actually see was our face.

I don't think we looked much like Romanian travellers on the trains, and we certainly didn't look like the gypsies that crowded every train station. But at least we didn't match the image of Westerners that Romanians sometimes saw in foreign films on the tightly regulated propaganda television in the country.

Students in our study groups noticed our poor clothes, but they never commented on how bad we looked, perhaps not fully understanding the reason for our intentionally shabby dress. However, occasionally a pastor who met us at the train

---

34 We always bought a tourist visa at the border when we entered the country. It was the only option we had, as all other types of travel were banned. In a limited way, tourism was welcomed because it generated money for the economy.

35 *Babushka* is the Russian word for *grandmother,* which was exactly how we felt when we wore this heavy scarf on our heads. The word had meaning for Romanians as well (they learned Russian in school), and they would laugh at our word for the heavy scarf.

station would thank me, after we arrived at his home, for our attempts to disguise that we were foreign travellers.

One day at coffee break during a long day of teaching, I noticed the students passing a little basket around the room, each woman putting a few *leu** into it as it made the rounds. Obviously, they were collecting money for someone. Filled with curiosity, I asked the translator what they were collecting money for. With great embarrassment she informed me that they were collecting money to buy me new shoes. "Yours look so bad, Miriam," she said. I felt like I was succeeding.

Historical Precedents

I received a letter from Magda the other day. She was one of my students thirty-five years ago in Romania. I treasure the eloquent letter in which she remembers the crazy travellers from the West who came to teach hidden groups of women during the difficult years under Ceausescu. Magda hasn't forgotten those days when we would arrive by train, dressed in our shabby second-hand clothes, hoping the secret police wouldn't pick us out of the crowd as foreigners. Her letter, painstakingly written in English, brought tears to my eyes:[36]

> Dear Miriam,
> Thank you for the humble way you came to us. We, your students, were the lowest in the poorest country among all the countries in Eastern Europe. I will never forget the old clothing you bought to look like us as much as possible, and the cheap bag made of woven plastic you would buy from the market so you would look even more like us. Even if all this was meant for your (and our) protection, you humbled yourselves so much to enter into our lives; in this way you got into our hearts. That was the first lesson we learned from you: to be humble before those you are ministering among.
>
> You, who could have remained at home in Canada in your cozy house, came to such a dangerous place where you risked being arrested along with us; you were an example to us. You took the risk for our sake, to feed our thirsty and hungry hearts. We Christians were so marginalized and despised by society; you opened our eyes to see who was on our side and who cared for us. You were an angel of God who came to strengthen us, to feed us, and to teach us how to withstand, no matter what would

---

36 Only an excerpt from her lengthy letter is posted here. I realize what an arduous task she undertook, writing her thoughts and getting them translated into English for me.

come upon our country or into our life. God built up a team of women all over Romania as an army which, growing in power, would defend their families and their children and support their husbands.

We embrace you with much love, gratitude, and appreciation.

—Magda

Magda's letter made me think about "identification"—radical identification. Identification happens when a person enters another culture,* develops a deep sense of belonging there, and is able to feel empathy with those around them. Barriers to effective ministry begin to disappear, and the people they hope to reach begin to accept them.

Identification doesn't mean that the newcomer abandons her own cultural identity, an approach sometimes referred to as "going native." Good identification leads to a bonding between the messenger and the newly adopted culture, because it means the newcomer has appreciation and empathy for the host culture—they identify with the people.

Jesus Became Flesh

Jesus is the best example of identification that I can think of. Consider the home he left behind in heaven. Imagine what it was like for the Creator and Sustainer of the universe to become a vulnerable, helpless human infant.

Scripture tells us that Jesus *"became flesh and took up residence among us"* (John 1:14, NET), or as another translation says, he *"moved into the neighbourhood"* (MSG). Jesus, who was fully God, entered so fully into human culture that he understood hunger and thirst, poverty and oppression. He cried when a dear friend died (John 11:1–44). He experienced rejection, anger, and loss. He knew what it was like to be bullied, and to see one of his best friends turn on him and deny him. There is nothing we humans experience that Jesus didn't. There was nothing too humbling for him to go through in order to bring us salvation. He had to become a human being in order to fully identify with human beings. He didn't just change his clothes—he came into the world through his mother's birth canal. Hebrews tells us that he was clothed in human flesh—he could empathize with human beings. Totally!

It's obvious, of course, that he didn't go to all this trouble for angels. It was for people like us, children of Abraham [which means children of Adam—that is, all human beings]. That's why he had to enter into every detail of human life. Then, when he came before God as high priest to get rid of the people's sins, he

*would have already experienced it all himself—all the pain, all the testing—
and would be able to help where help was needed.*

—Hebrews 2:16–18, MSG

True identification involves a lot more than just wearing clothes that are foreign to you. To really identify with people in a new culture, you have to first become a student of their way of life—jump into it with an open, trusting, and accepting outlook, being honestly curious and totally willing to learn how they live. If you're serious about identifying with people in the new culture, this first step will lead you to step two: participating with the people in their lifestyle and finding out what behaviour is culturally appropriate, without doing anything Scripture says is unacceptable.

It means trying to live without offense, living as a learner of culture, living with sensitivity to the situation in which you minister. These two important steps make it more possible to live with empathy and understanding in a different culture. You are learning to identify with the people. You begin to see the world in which you serve in the way that people you serve see the world. It doesn't happen overnight!

Some people refer to identification as "becoming like" the very people you want to introduce to Jesus. In order to communicate with us, Jesus became a human with flesh and bones, and blood coursing through his veins. For the sake of protecting the church in Romania from increased suffering because of my presence among them, I wore shabby clothes from the second-hand stores in Vienna. Hopefully I did a lot more than just change my clothes.

What About Head Coverings?

Churches have their own culture as well. During our first meetings in the early 1980s, we noticed something about the church culture of Romanians: every woman wore a scarf when they worshipped or prayed or read the Bible. It seemed to me that every group interpreted differently Paul's warning to women in 1 Corinthians 11:5 about praying or prophesying with her head uncovered. Some churches required a scarf be worn by all women in the church. Others thought it applied only to married women. Some thought scarves only needed to be worn inside the actual church building, while others wore scarves every moment of the day and night so they would never inadvertently shoot a prayer to heaven with an uncovered head.

Wanting to be culturally sensitive and to avoid offending my students, I always carried a tiny scarf in my bag, sometimes asking the women directly if I should put it on my head before I began to teach. In one group a woman told me directly, "No, you don't need to wear a scarf because you're not married!" In another group the women thanked me for my willingness to wear a scarf, because for them it spoke of my desire never to offend God—or my students. Over the years, as women became serious students of Scripture, I noticed more and more women came to class without scarves on their head.

I didn't care whether I wore a scarf or not. It just wasn't important enough to argue about, especially at the beginning of ministry in Romania. In my thinking, what Paul says in 1 Corinthians 11 about head coverings was addressed to women in a Jewish cultural context for a particular time in history, not to all women in all times and all places. But if someone held tightly to this part of their church culture, I would happily wear a scarf. It just wasn't a big deal.[37]

I really like how the Apostle Paul thought about culture as he travelled around in Asia on his missionary journeys. Paul didn't let himself be bound by the demands and expectations of everyone to whom he ministered. What he wanted most was to be heard—to get a hearing among all kinds of people. He spoke of voluntarily becoming a servant to those whom he hoped would hear his message:

> … *religious, nonreligious, meticulous moralists, loose-living immoralists, the defeated, the demoralized—whoever. I didn't take on their way of life. I kept my bearings in Christ—but I entered their world and tried to experience things from their point of view. I've become just about every sort of servant there is in my attempts to lead those I meet into a God-saved life. I did all this because of the Message. I didn't just want to talk about it; I wanted to be in on it!*
> —1 Corinthians 9:20–23, MSG (emphasis in original)

I didn't *have* to wear a scarf. But I wanted to enter their world and *become like* them in every way possible for the sake of my teaching. Another reason for wearing old clothes was so my students wouldn't be distracted by the trendy clothes of

---

37 Years later, my friend Sanda shared how hard it was for her to stop wearing her scarf in church, even after her congregation had wrestled with their understanding of Scripture on head coverings and released women from feeling obligated to wear them. Her hesitancy to stop wearing the head covering to church suggests that it had become an integral part of her own understanding of culture and an important part of who she was. It was pretty hard to give it up!

a visiting teacher from Vienna. I didn't want anything to ruin my chances of a good hearing of the Word

When I returned to Romania thirty-five years later, the women thanked me for honouring them in this regard in the early days. Over time, they began to understand and interpret the Scriptures for themselves. Their husbands noticed that we didn't suggest new ideas about head coverings. If we had, the women might have missed everything else we taught them, just because of the offence of our refusing to wear a scarf. It was such a simple way to identify with these women, and we discovered that it made them feel comfortable in our presence. If we had refused to humbly accept their church practice, they might have closed their ears to everything we were teaching.

Becoming Romanian in Every Way Possible

Our attempts to identify with Romanian women were very intentional. I asked Romanian women to tell me if anything I did was offensive in their culture. I wanted to see my behaviour while in Romania through their eyes.

I remember one day a woman told me that even the way I walked in the street gave away my identity as a Western woman. Sure, I might be carrying a *punga* (a cheap bag woven out of plastic, sold by the gypsies in the marketplace), but unfortunately, I walked with confidence and a spring in my step. She told me I needed to learn how to "plod" if I wanted my gait to coincide with the clothing of a poor, older woman. Old Romanian women always lean forward slightly as though the heavy bags they carry weigh them down. I had to even learn how to walk like an older Romanian woman if that was how I dressed!

Identification Has Limits

We tried to identify with Romanian Christians in every way possible when we travelled to Romania. But our identification had limits. I could observe but never fully identify with the harshness of the regime they lived under. For example, if our secret meeting was discovered by the secret police, I might be arrested. I would probably be questioned at police headquarters and then asked to leave the country with a notation in my passport that I could never return. That happened to several of my colleagues from Vienna, who were ordered to leave Romania with their passports stamped *persona non grata*. They were now marked as an unwelcome person in the country.

But for my Romanian Christian brothers and sisters, if my presence in their home was discovered, very soon after I left town, they would hear the dreaded knock at the door and the pastor or head of the household would be escorted to the headquarters of the secret police. Here they would be interrogated—sometimes for days, on occasion beaten to within an inch of their lives, and perhaps even sent to prison. Even if they were not physically harmed or imprisoned, they might be warned that the family's food ration allotment would be much smaller the next week, or the boss in the factory would try to find ways to intimidate them. A pastor who cared for multiple churches would find his gas rations drastically reduced the week after we left town, perhaps to fifteen litres a month. Surveillance of his family might be increased, and his children ridiculed in school.

It was hard for me to fully identify with what my presence in homes might mean for my Romanian friends. If I were arrested and interrogated, the secret police and I would both know that I carried a Canadian passport. I never underestimated the strength of that small but powerful document. Behind my passport stood the Canadian government and its commitment to me as a citizen under its protection. That made it hard to fully identify with Romanians in the unpredictable and cruel environment of a state that wanted to destroy the church and stamp out Christians. There were limitations to my identification with the everyday lives of my Romanian brothers and sisters.

Always a Foreigner?

I am on the train from Braila (Brăila) to Bucharest again. It's always a relief when the train finally leaves the station, because Braila is one of those small industrial cities that the secret police say tourists have no reason to visit. What interest could a tourist possibly have in Braila apart from visiting Christians? There are always secret police waiting on the platforms, watching the arrival and departure of trains, discovering who has been in the city for the night.[38]

Every seat in the second-class compartment is occupied by old but unfortunately very curious women. Some are on their way back to their village after spending the day selling their produce in the market in Braila. The luggage racks above our heads sag under the weight of their canvas bags. Any sacks that won't fit on the overhead racks are stacked on the floor in the middle of the compartment. My legs are buried up to my knees with canvas bags full of small animals, feed, fresh produce, and seeds.

As the train moves slowly along, I am becoming more and more uncomfortable, realizing that they intuitively know I am a foreigner. But how? I haven't said a word since entering the compartment, dressed in my old clothes and wearing the

---

38 Years later, when I read the secret police files on Pastor Joseph Stefanutsi (Iosif Ştefănuţi), I realized how often they noted that Stefanutsi had foreign guests, sometimes even noting "two foreign women" met him at the train station. Perhaps our disguise wasn't as good as we thought it was.

wool *babushka* scarf on my head. I think I look old and bedraggled, just like those sitting in the compartment with me. At least that's how I feel. Several days earlier, I even purchased a Romanian suitcase in an outdoor market. Today I carry the suitcase and a brightly coloured *punga,* a woven bag made by the gypsies. How do they know I'm not Romanian? But as they chat, I hear phrases like *"E străină,"* a word I know means "foreigner." I feel their inquisitive eyes as they turn and look at me.

I can't move my feet because they're trapped under the women's bags and dirty bundles. As the train moves slowly along, I realize that all eyes are on me as they discuss *"O femeie străină"* (the foreign woman). The woman on my left gently strokes the old and faded leather purse I bought at the thrift store in Vienna. She says softly under her breath, *"E atât de frumos!"*—"It's so beautiful!" Speaking loudly and using wild gestures, the woman sitting across from me by the window offers to exchange her faded and patched dirty jacket for the army-green wool coat I'd bought in Vienna. I thought the coat was rather severe looking. I assumed that since it was made in Austria, I wouldn't stand out on the streets of any European city. Wrong! An Austrian quality wool coat would be highly prized by anyone here who was able to buy it.

The woman on my right by the door becomes bolder by the minute. She reaches under the bundles in the middle of the compartment and rudely pulls my boot-clad right foot from under the pile of bundles. She lifts it high into the air so everyone can see it. She strokes the worn black boot, also purchased in the thrift store in Vienna for ten shillings (two dollars). I hear the word again, *"Frumos! Frumos!"*—"Beautiful! Beautiful!"

Overcome with curiosity, the old woman who holds my foot in the air even strokes the panty hose showing between the top of the boot and the hem of my skirt—and as she strokes my silky hose and looks around the compartment, they all mutter, with hushed amazement, that word: *"Frumos! Frumos!"*

I am frightened and sad that my disguise seems to have fooled no one. My attempts at "identification" seem not to be convincing—a sham! Perhaps it works in a crowded train station, but up close, anyone can see it is nothing but a disguise. As hard as I try, I will always be a foreigner.

Letitia's Story

Letitia (Letiția)'s heart pounded wildly with anticipation and lots of fear as she thought about what her husband had just told her. He'd whispered to her what the teacher from Vienna had told the men in his group—women from Vienna wanted to start a group for wives and a few other trusted women. What made Letitia's heart pound out of control was their request that her home be the meeting place for the women. She had a relatively new apartment that her husband, a builder, had made very beautiful. The apartment was on the second floor of a block of flats in a newer subdivision of Timisoara, a long way from the train station. It would be quite safe from the prying eyes of the secret police.

Such Handsome Men
Over the years, Letitia had opened her home to several of the Western men who came to teach the men's group. Sometimes she cooked a hot meal for them; sometimes she gave them a bed for the night. She smiled as she thought about the Americans who had stayed in their home—tall, handsome men, immaculately dressed in tasteful clothes and carrying only a small travel bag. A vision of what the wives of these handsome men might be like danced in her head—fashionably dressed, beautifully manicured nails on hands that had probably never handwashed sheets and towels in cold water. Their hair would be beautifully coiffed by a superb stylist, and tastefully applied makeup would make them even more breathtakingly beautiful.

Renovations at Home
Titi, as her friends called her, sprang into action as images of her future teachers filled her mind. She shared the exciting news with the woman who took care of her children while Titi, who had a reputation as somewhat of a "fashionista," worked at a bridal shop in town. Titi's nanny, who had once visited Western Europe, glanced around her apartment and without mincing her words said, "You have some work to do, my friend! This apartment needs a total renovation before you can host women from the West!"

Over the summer months of 1986, Titi and the nanny painted every room in the apartment. Carpets were taken outdoors for pounding and washing over the back fence. Curtains came down and were washed and ironed. Unfortunately, the fresh paint made her furniture look old and worn. Her friend told her it would have to be replaced. Each time Titi thought the project was finished, her friend would see something else that really had to be done in her home before the foreign women arrived.

The American Women Arrive
The day of the first meeting of the women's study group in Timisoara, October 1986, finally arrived. Titi awoke in the early morning with thoughts of the lovely women who by now were probably on a train somewhere between the Romanian border and Timisoara. They would arrive in the late afternoon for their first meeting.

Visions of their tasteful clothing, their beautifully styled hair, their manicured, brightly coloured nails, and impeccable makeup drifted through her mind again. Would they approve of her freshly decorated home?

At the agreed-upon hour, a man from her husband's group went to bring the travellers from the train station, escorting them by tram so that no one would suspect there were visitors in the apartment block. Titi knew the routines of connecting in the train station without alerting the station police of the arrival of foreigners. The precise signal—it might be a paperback in the hand of the traveller and a similar one in the hand of the person meeting them—would have been established months before when the meeting dates were agreed upon by all.

She smiled as she pictured these beautiful women following their contact out of the station to the tram stop without saying a word. The women would follow at a distance as their contact walked in ever-widening circles around the station, always checking over his shoulder to confirm they were not being followed, before stopping at the tram.

Titi heard the scrape of the heavy, ill-fitting door, one floor below her at the entrance to the building. She heard footsteps on the stairs and pictured her beautiful guests coming up the unlit stairwell to her second-floor apartment. She waited, knowing that the apartment door had been left unlocked so that her guests, led by their guide, could let themselves into the apartment without knocking. Her heart was pounding so loudly she was sure the neighbours must hear it as she waited just inside the door to greet her guests.

In the dark hallway, accompanied by their guide, stood two bedraggled women travellers with all but their faces covered by heavy scarves. Their coats were dull and shapeless. Their guide carried their bags which were made of dirty canvas. Each woman carried a *punga* they had purchased from gypsies in the market.

For just an instant, Titi stood frozen in the entryway as she thought about the newly renovated apartment just behind the living room door. The money and hours invested in renovations over the past six months flashed before her eyes. As she looked into the faces of the two strangers in the hallway, she thought to herself, "I did all *that* for *this*?" And then she opened wide the living room door and her heart to receive these travellers into her life.

Going Further: Recommended Reading
Elmer, Duane. *Cross-Cultural Servanthood: Serving the World in Christlike Humility.* Downers Grove, IL: IVP Books, 2006.

Lingenfelter, Sherwood G., and Marvin K. Mayers. *Ministering Cross-Culturally: An Incarnational Model for Personal Relationships.* 2nd ed. Grand Rapids, MI: Baker Academic, 2003.

Lambs Among Wolves:
The Local Church and Mission

CHAPTER FIVE

An Unusual Love Story

I had never been away from home in a permanent way. No one suggested I move out, but it was time. Time to explore who I was, without the expectations attached to my well-respected family name. Time to explore for myself who God was. Time to explore why the God of my fathers had created me. It was time to move out, with no plans to return.

I moved away from home to go to university. During my first weeks on the University of Calgary campus, I revelled in the anonymity that came with being one of ten thousand students. No one knew anything about me. I had a plastic ID card on which was my name, an ID number, and a ridiculous picture of myself. The card opened doors to lots of things around me. I loved the fact that I never bumped into preconceived expectations of how I should dress, how I should talk about God, where I should hang out with new friends, and what I should eat or drink with them in those places. Under the cover of anonymity, I began to explore my faith, identity, and life's purpose.

Very quickly I realized that I had inherited my father's love for language, which explained why the science of linguistics[39] captivated me. I was also fascinated by the French language. The combination of the two was a great fit for me. I chose to study linguistics and French.

I Fall in Love

On my first weekend in the new city, I wanted to meet new people. Someone told me about Foothills Alliance Church, just across the street from the university campus.

---

39 The scientific study of language. In my study I encountered many divisions of linguistics with strange names like morphology, syntax, phonetics, and semantics. I had to choose a modern language for the program. I chose French and got sucked into courses on how to teach French as a second language. That became my first career.

It seemed like a logical place to start. I walked through the church doors on the first Sunday morning in September 1971. In a sense, I've never left, though my career has meant I've been absent for years at a time!

Proximity to the university campus wasn't the only thing that explained the size of the young adult group there. The welcome Pastor Gordon and his wife, Eleanor, extended to everyone who came through the doors, and their encouragement to immediately get involved somewhere in the church, made this congregation a welcoming place for students like me who were looking for a church home.

It wasn't hard to find places to belong. I was quickly absorbed into music ministry, the College and Career group, and teaching Sunday school to grade five girls. I'd never experienced a church body that expected more of me than just showing up. I had grown up sitting in the family pew, watching a group of men (and very few women) "doing church" for the rest of us who sat and watched. Suddenly I felt like someone would notice if I didn't turn up. I began to believe I was an important part of the church that God was growing in the northwest corner of Calgary.

I found myself falling desperately in love with church. I would sit in the front row of the choir (in those days churches had choirs), feeling my heart would burst because of the love I felt for this new family that had embraced me. I was there every time the church doors were open. It was a safe place. I was needed. I was loved.

Even before graduating from university, I was offered a job in Calgary, teaching French and music in middle school. Professional life agreed with me and I found myself rising in the ranks of the school system. I enjoyed the freedom that came with a good salary, and quickly repaid my student loans. Professional life also allowed me to commit to even more involvement in this church that had become my life. Yes, I was falling deeper and deeper in love with a beautiful body of faith-filled people.

Somewhere far in the back of my mind was the day, nearly thirty years earlier, when at breakfast my mother had pressed me to tell my siblings that during the night I had invited Jesus into my life. The feeling I had as a seven-year old child still lingered with me—I knew I was a child of God, and I knew that God had something special for me to do. But I didn't know what it was! Reflecting on it now, it was (and still is) crystal clear that my call to follow Jesus was closely linked to a call to serve him.

My Gifts Are Affirmed

Jump ahead to a Sunday morning in spring 1978. Nearly seven years had passed. I will never forget arriving for church that day. The chairman of the elders, the men who led the church, met me at the front door and told me the elders wanted to speak with me after the service. My mind raced, a little bit anxious, trying to imagine why the church leaders might want to talk with me. As soon as the foyer of the church emptied that morning, a group of men gathered around me. Their spokesman asked a pointed question: "We're wondering if you plan to teach French the rest of your life."

His inquiry caught me off guard. He continued, "We've been watching you here in this church for seven years, and we believe, Miriam, that God has clearly gifted you for ministry. We think you should go to seminary and explore vocational ministry more intentionally."

I was shocked—speechless! The chairman continued, suggesting that I think about leaving my teaching job and going to seminary. I'd just paid off my undergraduate student loans. Seminary would be expensive, and I really didn't want to go into debt again. But their suggestion came with a surprising offer: "The church will pay your seminary tuition. While you're in seminary, if you discern that God has called you to a vocation of ministry, the investment we make in you will be an outright gift from the church. If you discern that God is not calling you to ministry, the investment we've made in you will simply be an interest-free loan."

As I walked to my car that morning, I was laughing and crying at the same time. *They think I have gifts for ministry! The church wants to help me explore if God is calling me to serve him in some ministry vocation! They believe it so firmly, they're willing to pay for me to go to seminary.*

Several months later I packed up my things, moved to another city, and became a student again, this time in a seminary (a graduate school where people are trained for ministry). My love affair with the church moved to another level that day. My congregation's leaders had launched me on a pathway to ministry that led me to Romania and later into pastoral and academic work that continues to this day. Their care for me now spans nearly fifty years. Their commitment to investing in young people in whom they see gifts for ministry is still strong, though happening in different ways today.

Time to Reflect

1. What missional issue does my story about Foothills Church raise in your mind as you think about taking the Good News to a hard place today?

2. Have you ever thought about the role a local church might play in the call of someone committed to doing mission? Do you have a personal example?

3. Where can you go to explore the issue more deeply? The Scriptures give us some examples of people who felt the call of God on their lives, whose gifts were affirmed by the local church, and were sent by a local church to work in a hard place.

Going Deeper

The Church Sends

It's been forty-two years since the leaders at Foothills Alliance Church tapped me on the shoulder and told me they saw gifts for ministry in my life. This is a memory that still fills me with awe. They launched me on a journey that gave me freedom and lots of confidence to pursue God's call. I knew that the church leadership had my back. They knew their young adults pretty well.[40] They watched us serving in the church. They tried to help us understand God's call in our lives. They had the courage to publicly affirm God's gifts and calling in our lives. Most importantly, they put their money where their mouth was, offering to help young adults like me financially if we were willing to explore the possibilities of vocational ministry. It has always felt to me like this local body of believers was functioning as God intends the church to function.

The Church in Antioch

The bold affirmation of the leaders at Foothills Alliance reminds me of a story in Acts 13. The story of the church in Antioch captures my imagination because it tells how Saul, who soon became known as Paul, was steered by his church from successful local ministries in Jerusalem (primarily among Jews) to taking the Good News to unreached people far away in the northern Mediterranean area. It's a fascinating example of a good church (yes, it reminds me of Foothills), with discerning leaders who understood God's call, and the important part the church plays in helping its own people to discern it. Here's how the writer of Acts described it:

> *The church in Antioch* had grown strong, *with many prophets and teachers: Barnabas, Simeon (a dark man* from Central Africa*), Lucius (from Cyrene* in North Africa*), Manaen (a member of Herod's governing council),*

---

40 I wasn't the only young adult that Foothills Alliance Church sent off to seminary. They identified and sent other young adults whom they thought were gifted and called—men and women who still give leadership to God's church in far-off places and in Canada. Most of us from the 1970s are approaching retirement now. But the leaders at Foothills continue to have a role in helping their people discern who among them will form the next generation of local church pastors and international workers.

*and Saul. Once they were engaged in a time of worship and fasting when the
Holy Spirit spoke to them, "Commission Barnabas and Saul to a project I
have called them to accomplish." They fasted and prayed some more, laid their
hands on the two selected men, and sent them off on their new mission.*

—Acts 13:1–3, VOICE (emphasis in original)

The church in Antioch must have been a happening place! Antioch was a
city of half a million people, a large urban centre in those days. It was a place that
was becoming more and more diverse. Syrians and Greeks, and before long many
more ethnic groups, were living inside the city walls. Historians speak of how each
ethnic group kept to themselves.[41] In Antioch there were thriving centres of learning, which probably meant the new church in town attracted lots of students who
were curious about "the Way," a new religion that had gained a following since the
well-known persecutor of Jesus-followers, Saul of Tarsus, had joined and become
one of the leaders. Antioch was a dark and desperate city in which the Good News
spread like wildfire. If you were a young adult who really wanted to worship Jesus,
the church in Antioch was the place to go. It sounds a lot like Foothills in the 1970s.

Early Christ-followers in this church were hard to describe. Most of them were
Syrians and Greeks, but people from other cultures who identified with Jesus also
found a safe place there. City authorities began calling them "Christians" (Acts
11:26), a nickname that had been flung by sarcastic men in Antioch at those who
worshipped in the church. It wasn't just a label for an emerging, identifiable group
that needed a new name. They were trying to find a way to describe these people,
coming from many ethnic groups in the city, who had one thing in common—they
followed Jesus Christ. The name stuck. Christ-followers willingly accepted it. The
decision to follow Jesus broke down the existing racial divisions. What they had in
common was far deeper than race or religious heritage. Their identity was in Christ,
and in Christ the walls that separated them came tumbling down.

Luke, who wrote the story in Acts, describes the church leaders in Antioch.
They certainly weren't the typical leaders you would find in the Jewish synagogue
in Jerusalem. Paul and Barnabas, two of the leaders, were Jews who had grown up

---

41 First-century historians tell us that the architects of Antioch designed the city with walls that would
keep ethnic groups from fighting each other. They identify as many as eighteen ethnicities that
lived in the city. We can appreciate in a new way Paul's reference in Ephesians 2:14–16 to Christ
*"destroying the dividing wall of hostility, making peace and reconciling people to each other through the
cross"* (NIV, slightly paraphrased). Those words would have special meaning to the multicultural
church in Antioch, where people came from behind walls in order to worship with people of other
ethnicities.

outside Palestine. Although Hebrew was the expected language of Jews, Paul and Barnabas spoke Aramaic and Greek more fluently than Hebrew. Manaen, another leader, was a man who had grown up in the household of Herod Antipas, probably in the lap of luxury and with an impressive education. Luceus of Cyrene was from North Africa. My guess is that he'd fled Jerusalem because of the persecution that ensued after Stephen was stoned there (Acts 7). Perhaps Luceus landed in Antioch as a migrant refugee. Then there was Simeon, likely a black man from Africa, whom they called "Niger."[42] This was a really diverse leadership team.

With such diversity among the leaders, imagine how hard it would be to agree on anything. When your leadership team is culturally diverse, it takes a lot more patience to reach consensus, if that's an important goal. These leaders didn't settle into a comfortable, tight group who loved working together and were content to see their congregation grow bigger and bigger. They could have done that. But the Holy Spirit was giving them a vision that went far beyond simply building a megachurch in Antioch. They dreamed of places where they could plant more churches. They had a global vision—beyond them in the world of the western and northern Mediterranean region, into Asia and all the way to Italy, there were unreached people groups who had never heard of Jesus. They wanted to bring these people access to him.

Imagine the disruption to their tight-knit leadership team when, one day as they were worshipping and praying, the Holy Spirit prompted them to set apart some of their team to take the Good News to those who had never heard of Jesus! The Holy Spirit told them he had a special project for which Barnabas and Saul were needed. In effect, the Spirit asked the church to release nearly half of their leadership team to the new project.

The Church Listens to the Spirit

The leadership at Foothills Alliance in 1978 wasn't quite as diverse as the lead team in Antioch in 40 AD, but as Calgary has become increasingly diverse in terms of culture, language, and race, leaders at Foothills have tried to follow the example of the church in Antioch.[43] The believers in Antioch understood that if God's plan was

---

42 In the original language, the word "Niger" is often translated as "black." Therefore, some scholars have concluded that Simeon "who was called Niger" was a black man, presumed to be an African gentile, transplanted to Antioch where he became a Christ follower. It is a reasonable conclusion.

43 Foothills Alliance in the 1970s was a predominantly monocultural church. In 2020, Foothills embraces diversity at every level—gender, age, culture, and language—with people on their team of pastors and elders from places like Nigeria, Malaysia, China, and Japan. The leadership includes women and men, older congregants and young apprentices who are learning how to lead.

that all nations[44] on earth should hear about Jesus and that a church should be established in all those places, their flourishing church would have to release some of its members to the nations.

Picture that prayer meeting in Antioch. People were worshipping and fasting. The presence of the Holy Spirit among them was unmistakably real. Scripture says the Spirit spoke, and the people in the meeting knew without any doubt what the Spirit was saying: "Set apart Barnabas and Saul for a project I have called them to accomplish." Perhaps someone objected because they knew how disruptive it would be to lose two of their finest leaders. That led to more fasting and prayer, maybe just to be sure they'd gotten it right.

I know by experience how Paul and Barnabas must have felt when the church went back to fasting and prayer. On the one hand, they felt a certain exhilaration in realizing that the church was "setting them apart," acknowledging their giftedness, affirming that God's call was on their lives. On the other hand, they must have felt apprehensive, asking themselves if they could trust their church to get it right. This wasn't a moment to trifle with the lives of two mature men whose ministry God was already blessing. It wasn't as though they were looking for a new job!

What About the Call?

Recently I spoke with Jill and Johann,[45] a young couple who came to the front of the church one Sunday after I preached on God's heart for all peoples—the nations. They seemed to be deeply impacted by the message. They shared with excitement their growing certainty, confirmed by my message, that God was calling them to return to Russia to start a ministry. They had spent several weeks there the summer before teaching English as a second language, and had fallen in love with the people and culture. They told me they planned to give up their jobs and go back to Russia, self-funded, to start a long-term ministry there. They were enthusiastic about sharing Jesus with Russian youth.

At face value, their vision was infectious. But it raised concerns in my mind. Issues of sustainable finance, a team to work with, guidance, and care for this young, inexperienced, and naive couple nagged at my mind. This wasn't the time or place

---

44 *Ethne* (or *ethnos*) is the Greek word in the New Testament which is often translated *nations*. It is the word from which we get the English word *ethnic*. For example, in Matthew 28:18–20, often called the Great Commission, Christ says to make disciples of all *nations*. The word he uses is *ethnos*, referring not to nation-states, but to ethnic groups—missiologists refer to them as *people groups*.

45 Names have been changed to protect identity.

to give a lot of advice to such well-meaning young people. But there was a problem I just had to mention. Russian is a really hard language to learn, and Russia is a hard place to live—I know, because I've lived there. I wanted to know about God's call upon their lives for the ministry they were describing—ministry in a hard place. When times get tough, they would need to know God had called.

I assumed the couple were members of the church where we were talking, but just to be sure, I asked where they went on Sundays. Very quickly they assured me they attended the church—not regularly, but whenever both of them had the day off. I asked how they contributed in the church's ministries. Neither had time for ministry because their jobs filled so much of their lives. This didn't seem important to them at all. Excitement about going back to Russia radiated from their faces. They were very certain God was calling them to go there.

A question was forming in my mind, which I asked before our conversation ended: "Do the leaders in this church know about your call to Russia? Who do you share life and ministry with among the people here in this church? Are there people who would wholeheartedly say, 'Yes, we agree that the call of God is on Jill and Johann to start a new ministry in Russia. Their spiritual gifts will be well used there'?"

Who Gets the Call?
Over the years, I have discussed God's call with young adults in lots of churches. They always ask about it. My experience with university students and young adults has taught me to suggest that the best way to discern a call to any ministry is to allow the people among whom you serve in the local church to affirm both your spiritual gifting and their own sense of God's call on your life. I'm not sure you can really know God's call with certainty unless you've worked alongside people in a local church.

> The best way to discern a call to any ministry is to allow the people among whom you serve in the local church to affirm both your spiritual gifting and their own sense of God's call on your life.

At the Christian university where I taught, whenever a student came into my office to explore issues of God's call, my first question was always about their church. "What church do you go to now? What ministries are you involved with there? Who knows you and can affirm what your spiritual gifts are?" That's where I always began.

If I saw they were sincere in their desire to know that God's call is on their lives, I would remind them that apart from the affirmation of a local body of believers, I wasn't sure they would know, with one hundred percent certainty, what God was calling them to do. This is one of the important pieces of knowing for sure. I'd tell them that the best thing I did in university was to get involved in a local church.

I have never once doubted the calling taking shape in my life that Foothills Alliance Church affirmed in me that day more than forty years ago. You could say that God's call to serve him came through Foothills Alliance Church, and that it was that local church that sent me into ministry.

The Church Sends

Barnabas and Saul were quite involved in the church in Antioch. They had moved there from Jerusalem—where they had successful ministries—to lead and encourage the young congregation. These two men loved the people in Antioch, and God blessed what they did there. It's interesting that God's call came to the church while they were worshipping and fasting. I bet Saul and Barnabas were glad they were around that day! They were there when the Holy Spirit spoke, so they heard him say, *"Commission Barnabas and Saul to a project I have called them to accomplish"* (Acts 13:2, VOICE). Since God might speak at any time, it sure makes me want to be in church when he does.

Because the passion of God for the nations already burned in their hearts, Saul and Barnabas suspected that God had something very special for them to do. Hearing the Holy Spirit's voice that day was probably the confirmation they needed before taking another big step. But Saul and Barnabas didn't just get up and go—they were sent by their church. Imagine how it felt as their friends and fellow worshippers gathered around them to bless their sending. This was a symbol that they weren't going alone—they were going as an extension of all those who laid their hands on them and prayed over them.

I'll never forget the day the church laid its hands on me and sent me to Romania. The church had my back—and I was accountable to the church. It was a holy moment!

Lambs Among Wolves

"The church has been a good husband for me, loving me, protecting me, providing for me, praying for me, and caring for me—things a good husband would do." For nearly four decades that has been my mantra. Millennials ask many questions when I make such an audacious statement! The unusual love affair with my church continues today, more than forty years since the day the leaders of Foothills Church tapped me on the shoulder and sent me to the nations. Knowing they love me so much has sustained me in some pretty hard places. I've felt alone and sometimes quite vulnerable (I tell those stories in the next chapter), but there has been a sustaining sense of security even in those times, because I felt the arms of Christ's body wrapped tightly around me.

The Church Sustains

Jesus didn't make it very easy to respond to his call to serve him. When he recruited and sent disciples into the harvest fields, the invitation wasn't attractive at all. Try to imagine what his call sounded like when he spoke these words to a group of recruits:

> *There's a great harvest waiting in the fields, but there aren't many good workers to harvest it…. It's time for you 70 to go. I'm sending you out armed with vulnerability, like lambs walking into a pack of wolves.*
> —Luke 10:2–3, VOICE (emphasis in original)

The lambs-among-wolves lifestyle isn't very inviting. I'm sure the hearts of the new recruits skipped a few beats when they heard Jesus describe it that way. What an ominous warning from the lips of the man who in another place called himself the Good Shepherd (John 10:11). What good shepherd would intentionally send a defenseless lamb right into the middle of a pack of wolves? What chance would the lamb have of surviving—let alone converting the wolves? It's a picture of vulnerability.

Jesus didn't leave his hearers guessing what he meant. He went right on to explain, in practical terms, what the lambs-among-wolves lifestyle looks like:

> *Don't bring a wallet. Don't carry a backpack. I don't even want you to wear sandals. Walk along barefoot, quietly, without stopping for small talk. When you enter a house seeking lodging, say, "Peace on this house!" If a child of peace—one who welcomes God's message of peace—is there, your peace will rest on him. If not, don't worry; nothing is wasted. Stay where you're welcomed. Become part of the family, eating and drinking whatever they give you. You're My workers and you deserve to be cared for.*
> —Luke 10:4–7, VOICE (emphasis in original)

Most mission organizations don't make such crazy demands when they're recruiting people, even for the hardest places in the world. Imagine those first missionaries leaving without a wallet (where would you carry a credit card or cash for an emergency?), no backpack (where would you carry a change of clothing and shampoo?), walking barefoot (that would surely attract unwanted attention to the messenger), and arriving at a door, asking if you can stay the night. For us, this just isn't a *normal* lifestyle. Today, *normal* means we bring loaded duffel bags with us to our new location. We find the safest neighbourhood to settle our family. We choose the most secure home we can find in that neighbourhood. We stockpile food for times of uncertainty. We prepare for every unpredictable situation that might pop up, limiting risk as much as we can.

Over and over, Jesus told his disciples that following him meant they would have to deny themselves and take up a cross (Luke 14:33). The word "deny" in Greek actually means "to disown utterly." The same word was used just before Jesus was crucified, when Peter denied he knew his Lord. He utterly disowned any relationship with Jesus. In the same way, following Jesus means utterly denying oneself and one's needs. It's not a very attractive invitation.

> Jesus calls his followers to think about their lives as having no value at all compared with what it means to follow him. The terms of his contract aren't easy. We literally place our lives in his hands.

Jesus calls his followers to think about their lives as having no value at all compared with what it means to follow him. The terms of his contract aren't easy. We literally place our lives in his hands, giving him full control of whether we live or die. We let go of everything—and rely on him—for everything. That's where the body of Christ, the church, comes into the picture.

Letting Go of Our Right to Stuff

Jesus told the first missionaries they couldn't take on their journey anything they could fall back on. We protest. What about the next meal? What about emergencies? What happens when my cloak begins to fall apart? What if I can't find a place to sleep at night? This isn't a normal approach to life. I can remember, as a child, listening to the reports of missionaries who stayed in our home. I felt sorry for these good people who had to ask God's people for financial support. It happened all the time.

Today, it makes a lot more sense to me. In fact, I think it's a biblical lifestyle. It's a life of relying on the Good Shepherd for everything. The workers Jesus sent out had to rely on him, which meant they had to believe that when they knocked on the door of a home in Palestine, someone would receive them, feed them, and give them a bed for the night. I'm sure that at times this hospitality stretched the receiving family who ended up feeding the hungry messengers. The hosts had to rely on God's provision just as much as the disciples had to depend on God.

It was always humbling when churches in Canada joined forces with me, providing what I needed for daily life in Europe. They would ask what I needed to set up the tiny apartment in Vienna that I called home. They helped me buy clothes and medication and shampoo—everything I needed for day-to-day life in Europe. They paid for the old clothes I bought in the second-hand stores in Vienna, but they also made sure I was dressed well when I returned to Canada on home assignment to speak in churches. They paid for my train tickets, visas, hotels—and, yes, even my ministry of condoms (see Chapter 3). The salary of an international worker was small, but my needs were more than adequately met by the church in Canada. They sometimes even included me in their family vacations when I was on home assignment. It was humbling.

Travelling around Romania in the 1980s was also a humbling experience—humbling, but not humiliating. It was humbling to receive nourishing meals at the tables of Romanian Christians who lived from month to month on meagre food rations. The winter of 1986 was especially grim. Government rations that winter were pretty basic: each person in a household received one hundred grams of butter, one half kilogram of flour, and one kilogram of meat each month. Milk could only be obtained for children up to one year of age. Beyond that, there was no milk for children. A small pig cost six months' wages. Things were still worse for believers, who were often penalized or even completely denied their ration cards. Sometimes when a Christian went to pick up the family's ration card for the coming month, he learned there was no card for them. The reason given? They were "repenters."[46] And yet they fed the travellers from the West.

One afternoon I rode around the countryside with Pastor Titus and his wife. They hoped to find vegetables for the upcoming winter. There was little they could buy. It caused a stir when it was announced that for the coming winter, rations would remain the same—especially once Romanians learned that last year's rations were now to last for three months, not just one.

When I asked Sanda where she got chicken for the delicious *ciorba* (soup) she served us, with a twinkle in her eye she spoke softly about the "Christian mafia" who had pooled their resources so she could feed the teachers visiting from the West. Years later, Sanda's two grown sons, Tiberius and Timothy, laughed as they told me how, as children, they would sometimes look out the balcony door and then run into the kitchen crying, excitedly, "Miriam is coming! Miriam is coming!" They thought they could trick their mother into cooking delicious meals. Their young

---

46 During the twentieth century, evangelical Christians were called "repenters," *pocăiții*. The term is still used, though it's maybe not as derogatory a label now as it was in those days. There were cultural Christians and then there were *pocăiții* who believed that a life of repentance was essential to the Christian life. This stands in distinction to the claim by Orthodox priests that the Church saves people by administering grace. For many years, "repenter" was almost a synonym for "evangelical."

minds realized, correctly, that when she cooked for guests from the West, the leftovers were tasty. Yes, it was humbling to sit alone in the living room and eat, knowing that Sanda and her five children would eat what we sent back to the kitchen uneaten.

As an international worker, I was also humbled by Canadians who made commitments to meet my needs. Sometimes, they didn't know where the resources to honour their commitment would come from. A ninety-year-old widow in my church in Canada gave to my mission support out of her meagre retirement income so I could continue in ministry. A successful businessperson saw the importance of giving to my support so that the nations would hear the Good News.

Each widow or business owner in Canada and each Romanian family that fed me lived in total dependence on the Good Shepherd. I always felt honoured by their sacrifice—and humbled. The Good Shepherd often asks recruits to relinquish their right to earn a salary and live in total dependence on the Body of Christ for the stuff they need.

Living in dependence on the Good Shepherd allows the church—Christ's Body in Romania or Canada—to share in the work God is doing among the nations. This mutual dependence on the Good Shepherd means that the one who is sent can never claim, "This is my work." They realize it is "our work"—the work of Christ's Body, which sends and sustains the one who goes.

When a person tells me that they feel called to the nations and they'll do anything God asks *except* ask people to give money, I read them the lambs-among-wolves story from Luke 10. To some new recruits, asking for money is humiliating. For me, it's humbling. The lambs-among-wolves lifestyle is usually more obvious in the lives of those who go, but I know people in Canada and in Romania who live in total dependence on the Good Shepherd so that they can support those whom God has called to go to the nations. They, like me, live like lambs among wolves.

Letting Go of Personal Ambition

What about my right to a career? Sometimes when I've prayed for God to provide something I need—or *think* I need—I've told myself, "I have a good education. I could earn a good salary and pay for this on my own!"

When Jesus called his disciples to follow him, they were all employed. They weren't standing around looking for something to do. Each one was busy earning an income. At least seven of the twelve were fishermen, earning an honest wage. Matthew was a tax collector for the Roman government. He probably earned a pretty good salary. Each of the disciples left employment and followed Jesus, meaning they no longer had regular income. Some of them were married, which meant their wives and children shared in the sacrifice. It was a necessary sacrifice.

Down through history, men and women have walked away from great careers because they sensed the call of God on their lives. They have embraced the lambs-among-wolves lifestyle, relinquishing their right to a career. They willingly accept a life of dependence, which they share with the Body of Christ, which also sacrifices in order to send them.

Robert Jaffray (1873–1945), one of Canada's great missionary heroes in the twentieth century, was born into a wealthy family. His father, the owner of *The Globe* (the newspaper that became Canada's *Globe and Mail*), intended to pass to Robert his wealth, power, security, and prestige. But Robert walked away from the status and comforts of a lucrative career to follow God to the nations. He spent his life sharing the Good News in hard places like China, Vietnam, and Indonesia. He died in a dirty Japanese prisoner of war camp in Indonesia two weeks before the end of World War II.[47]

Asian parents whose children relinquish their right to a good career in order to follow the call of God to the nations often grieve their child's decision. For the parents, it means the loss of prestige in a community that highly values a career as a doctor or lawyer. Gone is their hope of a child who will provide for them in old age. The call of God on a young person from an Asian community also has sobering implications for the parents who release them.

Letting Go of the Right to Security

When God calls someone to go to a hard place, where people have never heard of Jesus or where it's risky to talk about Jesus, they sometimes ask me, "Is it safe?"

My first reaction, which might sound dismissive, is to ask, "When is it *ever* safe to follow Jesus?" Of course, that isn't a satisfying answer to such an important question. None of us wants to think about the possibility of dying at the hands of violent people. My young friend was raped and left to die in a rice field in a developing country. Another was raped by a member of a militia and had his child. When I get to this aspect of the lambs-among-wolves lifestyle, I think about Christ's words about utterly denying oneself in order to follow him. It's not an easy invitation. It's not for everyone—just think of how even in Canada we want to live in a "safe neighbourhood." This way of life is for those who know the Good Shepherd has called them and is sending them—for those whose call is affirmed by the Body of Christ.

---

47 In the section at the end of the chapter called "Going Further: Recommended Reading," a book on the life of Robert Jaffray is listed.

One of my childhood heroes in mission, Dr. Helen Roseveare, worked for decades in the Belgian Congo[48] as a medical doctor. I remember her story of being brutally raped by rebel forces in the Simba uprisings in Congo in 1964.[49] People often asked her the "Is it safe?" question, assuming that because she was raped, she had, indeed, not been "safe." It appeared to her questioners, and perhaps even to her, that God had not been her protector in the face of such evil. Helen did not dismiss the "Is it safe?" question easily. Obviously she hadn't been "safe."

In the nights after being raped at gunpoint, she asked God "Why?" As she spoke about her right to security, I can never forget hearing her speak of God's response to that very legitimate question. He asked her, "Can you trust me with what has happened to you, Helen, even if I never tell you why?" God's word to her was, "Maybe you're asking the wrong question. The question you're asking is, 'Is it worth it?' The lamb, thrown by the Shepherd into a pack of wolves, asks instead, 'Is he *worthy*?'" For Helen, the "safety" issue was overshadowed by the wonder of the Good Shepherd's worthiness.

In my memories, Helen would follow her story of being raped with stories of how God gave her ministries of healing among many who live with tragedy in their lives, tragedies that have happened in places where it isn't safe. She would ask, "Is he worthy of that risk?"

The church sends. The church sustains. It is an unusual love story, where God's church loves, provides, protects, and prays for the lamb whom the Good Shepherd sends among the wolves. In hard places, there is no more secure place than under the watchful, caring eye of the Good Shepherd.

Passing the Baton

I have a friend in Canada. His name is Jake. He is a retired school principal, now in his eighties. Every time he sees me, he puts his hand in the air and expects a high five from me. To most people, Jake's high five is nothing unusual. It's the greeting he gives most people. But for me, it means much more. When Jakes gives me the high five, I feel like he's saying to me, "I handed it off to you, Miriam!" Jake was among the group of elders who stood in a circle around a young French teacher one day in

---

48 Now the Democratic Republic of Congo.

49 Helen Roseveare, *Give Me This Mountain* (Scotland: Christian Focus Publications, 2006). This is only one of her many books in which she shares this story. The account written here is based on my childhood memory of her remarkable story of five months among the "wolves" in the Belgian Congo.

the foyer of the church and asked, "Are you going to teach French the rest of your life, Miriam? You have gifts for ministry. We believe the call of God is on your life."

That day, Jake passed the baton to me! He and the leaders of my church passed the baton to lots of young adults in those days at Foothills. He passed the legacy of affirmation to me! Through the years, I have benefitted from the legacy of godly men and women who recognize the importance of passing insight and affirmation to the next generation. I too want to "hand it off" to the next generation in the remaining decades I have, and in doing so, fulfill the purposes of God in my life.

Going Further: Recommended Reading

Krishnan, Sunder. *Hijacked by Glory: From the Pew to the Nations.* 2014. Available through the National Ministry Centre of the Christian & Missionary Alliance in Canada, Mississauga, ON.

Tozer, A.W. *Let My People Go: The Life of Robert A. Jaffray.* Camp Hill, PA: Wing Spread Publications, 2010.

The Angel of His Presence:
Encountering the Supernatural in Mission

CHAPTER SIX

Your Maker Is Your Husband

The angel of the Lord is a guard; he surrounds and defends all who fear Him.
—Psalm 34:7, NLT

It's my thirty-fourth birthday. I'm travelling alone—not an enviable position for a woman in Romania. I've spent the whole day teaching a group tucked away in a small room at the back of the church on Popa Rusu Street here in Bucharest. I marvel at the willingness of these women to travel across the country by train to meet for two days of classes together. As soon as class is finished, they pack their small bags. They will take the night train back to their towns, some to return to factory jobs tomorrow morning. They know that I, too, am travelling alone, and several of them offer to walk with me to the hotel through the dark—there are no streetlights on the sidewalks. On this night, my birthday, their care touches me deeply.

We walk in silence. We dare not speak in case the secret police are following us, maybe using their listening devices to eavesdrop on our conversation. We stop in the shadows of the huge oak trees across from the hotel, where we embrace. *"Pace,"* "Peace," we murmur to each other. I can feel the women waiting as I cross the street alone. They watch until they know I am safely through the front door of the hotel.

I enter the hotel and immediately sense something unusual. The lobby is swarming with men in army uniforms. The sound of Slavic voices tells me they are Bulgarian or Russian.[50] Perhaps they're soldiers on their yearly leave from military posts somewhere in the Soviet Union. I cross the busy lobby, hoping no one will notice me, and call the elevator. When the door opens, it's filled with more men in

---

50 Romanian is a "Latin" language, one of several European languages in the family of "Romance" languages with Latin roots. Romania is described as an island of "Latinity" in a sea of Slavic countries. The lovely, singing nature of the language is in stark contrast to the guttural-sounding Slavic languages of surrounding countries.

military uniforms. They push to the back to make room for me. Not a man gets off. I can smell liquor on their breath as they press in close.

I've briefed many women travellers in the past about what to do in such a moment: "If the elevator has unruly men in it, don't announce your floor by pushing the actual number. If you feel unsafe for any reason, push a number above or below your floor and walk some stairs to get to your room."

In the confusion of the moment I foolishly push the button for the seventh floor—the floor where my room is. The elevator rises slowly. The door opens, and I step into the hallway as a soldier props the door open with his heavy army boot. The men leave the elevator with me. They stand in silence and watch as I walk down the hall to my room, unlock the pitiful plywood door with its meaningless lock, and let myself in.

My heart is pounding. My head tells me I've done everything I always tell travellers not to do. The cheaply constructed plywood door mocks me as I drag a small desk in front of it and pile several chairs on top. At least if someone breaks into my room, they will first have to deal with furniture piled against the door.

I prepare for bed, repack my suitcase for an early morning departure, and crawl into the sagging little bed. Ten minutes later, there's a loud knock at the door. I hear the raised voices of men, calling out in a language I don't understand. They pound on the plywood. The sound of their voices rises higher and higher when I don't respond. The feeble excuse of a door shudders with every blow. If these are the men from the elevator, I imagine they might have gone down to the hotel bar for a few more drinks before someone suggested they visit the foreign woman staying in room 706.

I can see the creeping light in the hallway from my bed. It streams through the bulging crack between the door and the doorframe. A wider frame of light appears every time the men pound. Drunken voices rise as they continue to assault the door.

I lie there, lifting a prayer to God in a whimpering complaint, "Lord, this is why I need a husband!" Immediately I think of a passage from Isaiah I read earlier today:

> *Do not be afraid; you will not be put to shame. Do not fear disgrace; you will not be humiliated…. For your Maker is your husband—the Lord Almighty is his name…. Though the mountains be shaken and the hills be removed, yet my unfailing love for you will not be shaken nor my covenant of peace be removed, says the Lord, who has compassion on you.*
>
> —Isaiah 54:4–5; 10

There are no mountains or hills in sight—after all, I am buried under the covers—but the door is shaking. Over the noise and confusion in the hallway, God's Spirit speaks words of comfort to my own spirit: "Can I be your husband? Can I take care of you tonight?"

I lie back on the pillow. It seems the men have settled on the floor outside the door, hammering on it from time to time and calling out drunkenly until their voices begin to fade. But the feeble excuse of a door and its cheap little lock hold firm all night. I fall soundly asleep.

I wake up at 4:00 a.m to silence, get dressed, pack my things, and leave the hotel for the North Train Station. I need to be there early enough to get a ticket for Braila. A thought begins to run round and round in my mind as the taxi heads to the station: "... the angel of the Lord is a guard; he surrounds and defends all who fear him" (Psalm 34:7, NLT).

I am comforted by the Presence.

Time to Reflect

1. What missional reality does this story raise in your mind as you think about taking the Good News to a hard place today?
2. What do you already know about this reality? Do you have a story to tell that illustrates it?
3. Where can we go to explore this reality more deeply? The next section will help you think about the issue: the role and importance of the supernatural in ministry through the lenses of Scripture and theology.

Going Deeper

I believe in angels because the Bible speaks about them a lot, and also because God has sent angels to protect me in dangerous situations. I'll tell you a few stories about those experiences. If God asks you to take the Good News to one of the hard places in today's world, you will need to understand clearly the role the supernatural plays in the unseen battle between good and evil. There may be times when God sends angels to protect you, and you're going to need them! What is more, He might send angels to convince your listeners that your message is true.

When I talk to children, they often want me to tell them about my encounters with angels in communist Europe during the 1980s. I especially like to tell those stories to children, because they're constantly bombarded with images of the ghoulish and sinister in life: witches, goblins, and frightening creatures. I want to fill their minds with reminders that there are angels who hover over God's children. The Bible clearly tells us that angelic beings, quite distinct from God and from us humans, really do exist. There are friendly ones and hostile ones.

Take a look at the magazine rack the next time you check out at your local grocery store. Stories about encounters with angels are all over the covers of popular magazines. Unfortunately, some who record their stories of angelic deliverance cannot explain their miraculous deliverance from danger other than through imaginative speculation and a lot of fanciful guesswork, often rooted in New Age[51] understandings.

When I talk about angels, I don't want to go beyond what the Bible teaches about them and what they do. On the other hand, I don't want to follow the example of some who call themselves Christians but don't really believe the Bible. They speak of angels as nothing but superstitious ideas. They ignore truths from the Bible that clearly explain why God created angels[52] and how important angels are in taking the Good News to people who have never heard about Jesus. Unfortunately, even some rather good Biblical scholars who believe in the existence and work of angels relegate this part of theology to the margins of Christian thought, as though it's not really all that important to the Christian's task. Their treatment of angels doesn't do justice to what the Bible teaches about these creatures either. So, be very careful what you choose to read about angels today.

One of the books on angels I recommend to people going to hard places is Jerry Orthner's *Angels: Friends in High Places*.[53] Jerry's book explains in very accessible and sometimes humorous language what theologians refer to as "angelology" or the study of angels. Unfortunately, some theologians describe angels with big words that most of us can't understand. Jerry, who is one of my pastors at Foothills Alliance Church, talks about how people today are fascinated with these ethereal beings. He wonders if people are so fascinated by angels because they are hungry for spiritual things—really searching for God.[54] There are lots of Christian books that talk about

---

51 The term "New Age" usually refers to a mixed bag of cultural attitudes that blossomed in late twentieth century Western society, adapting ancient and modern cultures that emphasize beliefs like reincarnation, holism, pantheism, and occultism. These beliefs really don't belong within the mainstream of Christian thought. They are understandings that advance alternative approaches to spirituality that focus on right living and health.

52 For example, David F. Strauss, who wrote *Die Christliche Glaubenslehre* in the 1840s (Vol. 1 (Charleston, SC: Nabu Press, 2012), p. 670–671), wrote about angels but ignored what the Bible says as he tried to make sense of them.

53 Jerry Orthner, *Angels: Friends in High Places* (Carmel, NY: Christian Publications/Guideposts, 1997).

54 Ibid., p. xvi.

angels, Satan, and demons, capturing the undiscriminating imagination of people who really don't know their Bible. Unfortunately, even these Christian books offer lots of speculation, because they aren't grounded in the Bible. Jerry's book is an excellent read, and it is deeply rooted in what the Bible says about angels. He claims that everything we need to know about God and ultimate truth, including the truth about angels, can be found in the Bible, which he uses to answer many questions people ask about angels.

For example, people wonder, "Where did angels come from?" Angels were created by God, just as humans were. In Colossians we read, *"For everything, absolutely everything, above and below, visible and invisible, rank after rank after rank of angels—* everything *got started [was created] in him and finds its purpose in him"* (Colossians 1:16, MSG, emphasis in original). Angels are personal beings created by God.

To the question, "How many angels are there?" Jerry's answer is "More than four." His advice is, "Don't even try to figure it out. You can't count that high!"[55] Whatever the number is, the writer of Hebrews, whom Jerry says "stops the guessing," speaks of *"an innumerable company of angels"* (Hebrews 12:22, NKJV). That means you just can't count them.

To the question, "What are angels like?" Jerry tells us that they are "not mechanical, serial-numbered cosmic robots programed for windup search and rescue (or destroy) missions." They are personal beings with all the traits of personality that you and I have: intelligence, will, and emotions.[56]

They're intelligent. Daniel, who was a long way from home, sent by God to serve him among the nations, described how an angel came to him *"in swift flight about the time of the evening sacrifice. He instructed me [Daniel] and said to me, 'Daniel, I have now come to give you insight and understanding'"* (Daniel 9:21–22). One day, you might need the wisdom of an angel when you bump up against a really difficult situation in one of those hard places among the nations. Don't forget that angels are smarter than you are!

Angels have a will, the capacity to make choices, just like human beings do. Sometimes angels (and humans!) make good choices; sometimes they make bad ones. God appealed to the will of angels when he said, *"Let all God's angels worship him [Jesus]"* (Hebrews 1:6). He wasn't telling them they *had* to worship. Angels can choose whether or not to worship God—he has given them free will.

Lucifer, who at one time was an angel, rebelled and chose not to worship God. He took one third of God's angels with him right out of God's heaven. Using a

---

55   Ibid., p. 15.
56   Ibid., p. 16.

graphic metaphor, John describes Lucifer's fall: *"Its tail swept a third of the stars out of the sky and flung them to the earth.... The great dragon was hurled down—that ancient serpent called the devil or Satan, who leads the whole world astray. He was hurled to the earth, and his angels with him"* (Revelation 12:4, 9). Angels aren't robots. Like the dragon himself, they have free will when it comes to serving God.[57]

Angels have emotions. The Bible says that angels sang together at creation (Job 38:7). Can you imagine the singing and exuberant celebration? Jesus said there is also rejoicing in the presence of the angels of God when just one sinner repents (Luke 15:10). Angels can be happy—they rejoice when a human chooses to follow Jesus, to become a child of God.

The question I am asked most often is, "So, what do angels do?" The primary job of God's holy angels is to take care of Christians. That should be really encouraging to you if you are a Christ follower. In fact, Scripture seems to indicate that angels are assigned to specific believers and sometimes refers to "guardian angels" (see Genesis 48:16; Daniel 10:21; 12:1; Matthew 18:10; Acts 12:15). In some cases, angels team up with other angels to care for certain individuals or to intervene in difficult situations (Psalm 91:11–15).

But it gets even better. Hebrews 1:14 is a huge encouragement to me when I'm trying to share Good News with someone in a hard place. It says, *"What role then, do the angels have? The angels are spirit-messengers sent by God to serve those who are going to be saved"* (TPT). Imagine, angels serve *"those who are going to be saved."* Scripture and history are filled with stories of angels helping Christians. But this verse excites me so much, because it seems that angels also help people who are not yet part of the family of God. Angelic visitations may be what are needed to convince unbelievers about God's existence and his constant care for his children. Perhaps because of an experience that can only be explained as "miraculous," they will be drawn toward my wonderful friend called God. Remember the story of Cornelius in Acts 10? He was a high-ranking official in the Roman army, a man who believed in God, prayed regularly, and did all kinds of good things among the poor. But he wasn't yet a child of God. It took an angel from God (described as a *"man in shining clothes"* in verse 30) to connect Cornelius to Peter, who in turn introduced him to Jesus.

I often pray for my sixteen-year-old Muslim friend as I drive him to his soccer games. He doesn't much want to hear about Jesus, God's Son, who died to pay for his sins. But Hebrews 1:14 gives me hope. Maybe an angel will appear to him and validate in some way that everything I've told him is absolutely true. He's heard me explain that I am a child of God because I have accepted God's provision through

---

57   Isaiah 14 tells the same story very graphically.

the death of Jesus on the Cross. Hebrews 1:14 uses the words *"those who are going to be saved"* to describe those who aren't yet God's children. I've asked God to send an angelic messenger to convince my soccer-loving friend that everything I've told him is true. Right now, he doesn't believe me—but he might if an angel spoke to him.

> Be encouraged, because he may send angels to convince unbelievers that everything you say about the God of the Christians and his Son, Jesus, is true. Angels care about those who are not yet saved.

If God calls you to one of those hard places in the world—to people who are blind because of Satan's lies, even to people whose current belief system is hostile to Jesus—you will never be alone. God will send *"angels with special orders to protect you wherever you go"* (Psalm 91:11, TPT). And be encouraged, because he may send angels to convince unbelievers that everything you say about the God of the Christians and his Son, Jesus, is true. Angels care about those who are not yet saved.

I Am Sending an Angel Ahead of You

As I said before, I believe in angels for two reasons: because the Bible says they exist to protect God's people, and because I have personally experienced their care for me in times of danger. I began thinking about angels a long time ago. The first time I really grasped God's promise of personal angelic protection was a year before I moved to work in Romania. One morning while I was still in Canada, I was reading my Bible. The phone rang. It was Arnold Cook, the leader of the mission I wanted to work with, calling to tell me the mission would send me to Romania as an international worker. That was such good news!

When my excitement settled down, I went back to the chapter in Exodus I had been reading when the phone interrupted me. The words jumped off the page as I imagined what ministry in communist Romania might be like:

> *…I am sending an angel ahead of you to guard you along the way and to bring you to the place I have prepared. Pay attention to him and listen to what he says. Do not rebel against him; he will not forgive your rebellion, since my Name is in him. If you listen carefully to what he says and do all that I say, I will be an enemy to your enemies and will oppose those who oppose you. My angel will go ahead of you…*
>
> —Exodus 23:20–23

The verses were a confirmation that God was going ahead of me to a country that I knew was hostile to Christians, and wouldn't be happy about someone coming from Canada to work with the local church. God was opening the door for me to serve him in Romania, a communist country with an evil president, Nicolae Ceausescu. I didn't know yet that the decade ahead, the 1980s, would be the darkest decade in history for the church in Romania. But because of God's promise that day, I wasn't surprised when I encountered angels along the way, guarding me on my journey. When I stumbled, they were there to catch me. Their job was to keep me from falling (Psalm 91:12, VOICE). And they did!

The Angel of His Presence

I lean into the icy wind of the early morning as I climb the steps of the train station in Braila. My bags feel heavy as I struggle to balance them. I'm still travelling alone—not an enviable position for a woman in a country that is growing more desperate with each passing year. But I'm still strangely comforted by my experience of his Presence three days earlier in my hotel room in Bucharest.

Now it's 6:15, and already the station is crowded with people. Peasants are going to their fields in nearby villages with their wooden farm tools. Gypsies huddle together to keep warm. Military men in faded uniforms, sad-faced men and women—all bent on going somewhere on this early winter morning.

It has been a few tension-filled days in Braila, this town tourists are forbidden to visit. My heart aches for the believers here, who seem to be constantly under secret police surveillance. Their pastor, Joseph Stefanutsi (Iosif Ştefănuţi), deals every day with the threats and indignities of the police.

The women met for hours of teaching over the weekend, and I'm weary because I did all the teaching myself. The prospect of this last train back to Bucharest and a flight from there to Western Europe is a happy one. The travel connections in Bucharest will be tight, but not impossible—if my train from Braila arrives in the capital on time. I check the crude, hand-painted departure board to verify the train's schedule—arrival at 6:23 on platform two, and departure for Bucharest at 6:25. Only two minutes in the station! It feels too tight.

The icy wind and an awareness that the platforms in Braila are always patrolled by secret police convince me to wait in the smoke-filled waiting room rather than on platform number two. The task of the secret police is to search the faces of travellers, looking for people like me who have no permission to be there. There will be time enough to cross the empty track on line number one to platform number two once I hear that the train is arriving.

At 6:23, I hear the muffled announcement of the accelerated train to Bucharest arriving on track number two. As I gather my bags and leave the waiting room, I see that another train has pulled into the station on track number one, loaded with passengers. I hadn't expected that! The train blocking my way is a *tren personal*, a second-class local train that will stop in every little village to drop off or take on workers going to the fields, or people just needing to get to a nearby village. The entrance to every car is packed with gypsies and peasants with their wooden tools, pigs, chickens, and stacks of dirty bundles filled with produce.

Instantly I realize my predicament. The train that is now stopped on track number one—right in front of the station—blocks my access to the train that is pulling into the station on track number two.

The train on line one is far too long to walk around in two minutes. Nor can I imagine hoisting myself and my bags onto the crowded train on line one and pushing through the people, animals, and bundles to jump down on platform number two. I might get caught by all the people packed into the first train, or it could begin to move at any moment, with no telling where it might be headed.

By now the train on line two has halted for its two-minute stop. Time is short. Seconds seem like hours as I realize the impossibility of my situation.

> With a silent scream, my fear is voiced to the Father. *Lord, help me!* Instantly, a man is at my side.

With a silent scream, my fear is voiced to the Father. *Lord, help me!* Instantly, a man is at my side. He takes my bags from my hands. I have no idea how he knows what I need, but he says only two words, "Follow me!" (I can't remember, now, if he said them in English or in Romanian. I only know I understood.) He climbs without hesitation into the seething train on line one. I follow, climbing the stairs into the crowded space between two cars. Like the waters of the Red Sea for the Israelites, the crowd parts as we push through.

As I descend onto platform number two, I see the train for Bucharest slowly beginning to move out of the station. I run—fast! The man carrying my bags runs behind me. I climb the stairs as the train picks up speed, and the man hands me my bags, which I turn to put down in the entrance between two cars. I turn back to thank my helper, but the platform is empty. The man is nowhere to be seen.

As I sink into a seat in a compartment filled with people and bags, my mind turns to the man who just helped me. Who was the helpful man who had seen and understood my predicament? Where did he come from, and where did he disappear to in an instant? As the train gathers speed toward the capital city and my flight to Vienna, I am again aware of a wonderful Presence.

Listen to What He Says

Three and a half years later, I am back in Braila, the same bleak city where it seems the battle with evil is particularly intense. Pastor Joseph seems so discouraged tonight as my travelling companion, Grace, and I arrive. Perched in the crowded little sitting room of their apartment above the church, I watch as the pastor's wife, Mia, piles pillows on top of the telephone on the floor. She gestures, pointing first to the pillow-covered phone and then, with her hands cradled like a telephone to her ear, silently mouthing, "They are listening to us!"[58]

As we visit, Pastor Joseph whispers that a church in Comanesti (Comăneş-ti), about two hundred kilometres away, was bulldozed by the authorities the night before.[59] Even while he is speaking, from beneath the pile of pillows we hear the muffled sound of the phone ringing. When Pastor Joseph gets off the phone, he tells us that the call was from the pastor of the demolished church in Comanesti, calling from prison where he and eight of his elders have been taken. He is asking if Joseph can come to Comanesti to plead on their behalf with the authorities. Joseph has promised he will come tomorrow.

Grace and I will spend the night in the dingy hotel where I often stay. Since Pastor Joseph needs to go to Comanesti tomorrow to help the believers waiting in prison, I assure him that we can walk to the church tomorrow for the 1:00 p.m. meeting with the women. It's only a twenty-minute walk—one that I've done several times before, right down Republicii Street,[60] the main street of town. It's a pedestrian-only walkway, which for many months has been torn up while new paving stones are put in place. I'm very certain I can find my way to the church from there.

The next day, we are cautiously picking our way along the uneven surface on Republicii Street. The pedestrian part of the street, which is still under construction, narrows to allow for only one person at a time to walk along planks laid in the mud. We stand back and wait before stepping onto the plank, watching a frail old lady,

---

58 Years later, when I read the secret police files on Pastor Joseph, I realized that every conversation we had in the tiny apartment of the Stefanutsi family was meticulously and laboriously transcribed by hand by eavesdroppers in Securitate Central via a "bugged" phone in the apartment.

59 The story of the destruction of the church in Comanesti is told in the next part of this chapter.

60 Now called, depending where you are on the street, either 1 Decembrie or Mihai Eminescu Street.

holding tightly to the hand of a young woman, walk toward us on the plank. As they pass us and continue down the walking street, my eyes briefly meet those of the young woman helping the old lady. I can hardly remove my gaze from her incredibly kind face. She wears large horn-rimmed glasses which make her face unforgettable. She passes us, gently depositing the old lady on a more even part of the walkway.

We begin to carefully inch our way along the stretch of plank the two women have just left. I am aware, however, that the young woman has left her companion, turned around abruptly, and is now following us as we try to walk along the plank, balancing by clutching each other's hands.

She is approaching us when I hear her loudly clear her throat three times. I turn, hoping not to lose my balance, wondering why she is making that noise. It seems to be an attempt to get the attention of someone ahead of her. My eyes meet hers, which she fixes on me as she wildly gestures with one finger to turn right. She seems to be telling me to get off the street by going right immediately, but she is a total stranger, so I assume the signal is for someone else.

We continue to walk precariously along the plank. Now she is close behind us, loudly clearing her throat again—three exaggerated, staccato coughs. Again, I look behind me. My eyes meet hers. With a pleading look, she gestures with her finger for us to turn right, into the side street we are approaching.

By now Grace is aware of her too. "Is she telling us to get off this main street?" Grace whispers.

"Or," I whisper back, "is she luring us down this side street where someone will rob us?"

By now, both of us are also wondering if the pastor has sent her to warn us not to go to the church! Again, the woman clears her throat three times. When I turn once more, she places two fingers on her right hand in front of her eyes as though to say, "Someone is watching you!" At the same time, with the other hand she points with desperation down the street to our right. Her eyes seem to plead, "You must obey me!"

I feel compelled to obey. At the end of the plank, we turn to the right off the walking mall and make our way down the side street to which she has pointed. I turn to see if the woman is following us, but there is no one in the intersection.

Having turned off the familiar street, I am now in unfamiliar territory. Once in the back streets, I feel absolutely lost. We wander, not knowing where the church is or where we are, getting more and more lost at each street corner.

After nearly an hour, I suddenly see familiar landmarks and I know we are close to the church. When we ring the bell on the gate, Pastor Joseph opens it and motions us quickly into the courtyard. His face is drawn and white. He leads us without a word up the stairs to the little apartment above the church.

"I thought you were going to Comanesti. Why are you still here?" I ask when he closes the door. Without giving him a chance to respond, I continue, "Did you send someone to the main street an hour ago to tell us not to come here?"

His face is full of surprise. I describe the kind-faced young woman with big glasses. No one in his church matches the description. He goes on to tell us that during the preceding hour, he had interactions with the secret police in the street right in front of the church. The Securitate had been waiting for him to leave the church at noon. Of course, the authorities knew of his plan to go to Comanesti today, as they were eavesdropping on the plea for help from those in prison last night.

One hour before, as Joseph was leaving for Comanesti, he was pulled over by police before he could even cross a single intersection. He was accused of stopping with the nose of his car a few inches into the crosswalk, a trumped-up charge for which they took his driver's license from him for three months. As he sat in his car, waiting for them to write up his ticket and a summons to court, he realized he could not drive to Comanesti today. He began to pray that his foreign visitors wouldn't walk down the street and ring the bell on the church gate at one o'clock. That would give the police an even greater reason to arrest him. As he sat waiting for the ticket, he pleaded with God to delay our arrival at the church.

My mind is filled with questions again, and an awareness of a warm, protective Presence descends on me. Did God send his Messenger to redirect the path of his servants? Is the kind-faced woman with the big glasses one of an angelic order in this town—a Messenger whose mandate it is to keep God's servants from harm? All afternoon, I feel the intensity of a battle with evil. But as we make our way through the dark streets to the hotel later that night, it seems that angels hover over us as we retrace our steps along the torn-up surface of Republicii Street. I feel the closeness of the Presence once again. He spoke. I listened.

Meanwhile in Comanesti…
Years later, I learned the story behind my second angelic encounter in the streets of Braila. In my research, I discovered a faded, almost illegible clipping from a Baptist journal of thirty years ago with the story behind the story, details I might never have known otherwise.[61]

---

61 The details of the demolition of the church in Comanesti appeared in the *Baptist Press* of April 16, 1990, the news bulletin of the Southern Baptist Convention, Nashville, TN.

On May 31, 1989, one day before my angelic experience in Braila, one hundred uniformed policemen arrived at the beautiful, newly-constructed church in Comanesti. It had taken the one hundred and twenty believers in Comanesti nine years to build the church. With several bulldozers and other heavy equipment, the police demolished the recently completed building. Eight of the church's leaders, including their pastor, Ionel Chivoiu, were arrested. Some were detained for a few hours until the demolition was finished. A few, including the pastor, were imprisoned for three days. They were beaten, and four of the leaders received a sentence of one to three years of hard labour on government farms. The church was told that their families would have to provide for family members in prison. Needing support and advice, Pastor Chivoiu called Pastor Joseph from prison. His phone call came while I sat in Joseph's living room on May 30.

Several young adults among the youth group in Comanesti went to the site that May morning in a brave attempt to try to stop the demolition. They were immediately arrested and jailed for a short time. An agent of the secret police warned the father of one of the youths who was in prison that Ceausescu's government was determined to "exterminate all Baptists."

On a trumped-up charge, believers in Comanesti were accused of using illegal building materials to finish the church. Ceausescu's agents claimed to have an anonymous tip accusing the church members of obtaining supplies from "private sources" rather than buying everything from state-run suppliers. The secret police hated Pastor Chivoiu, who pastored several churches in the area. They hated him because they saw his ministry was exploding—believers knew his ministry in their churches was anointed by the Spirit. The authorities grabbed any excuse to destroy him. That day, Pastor Chivoiu phoned from prison in Comanesti to the only person he could think of—his mentor, Pastor Joseph in Braila.

Six months later, near the end of December 1989, Romanians realized that a revolution was unfolding in their country. Courageously, Romanians began to believe that the evil regime of Nicolae Ceausescu was perilously close to toppling. On Christmas Day, 1989, from the balcony of his apartment building in Bacau, Pastor Chiviou announced some startling news to the waiting crowd below: Ceausescu's reign of terror was finished. Chiviou led the youth group in public prayers of thanksgiving for God's intervention on behalf of his people, delivering them from the evils of the communist regime.

Five Years Later—1993

A few years later, the phone rings in my garret apartment in Chicago. A woman introduces herself as Ruth, a nurse at Sacred Heart Medical Center in Spokane, Washington. She reminds me that we were neighbours in Canada during our childhood.

One of her patients in the cardiac ward at Sacred Heart is a pastor from Romania who has had a heart attack while visiting Spokane. Ruth sees his loneliness in a foreign country while experiencing great physical challenges and having minimal English. She casually mentions to him that she prayed for years for a Canadian woman who worked in Romania during the 1980s. To her surprise, the patient, Joseph Stefanutsi, calmly asks, "Was her name Miriam?" With a little sleuthing, Ruth finds my phone number and connects us by phone.

My heart fills with joy as I tell Pastor Joseph my angel stories that happened in his home town of Braila. At the end of my stories, he calmly replies, "Miriam, in the difficult years during the communist regime there was such a battle between the unseen powers of good and evil in Braila that we expected angels to turn up, to intervene on our behalf in those dark days."

If God calls you to serve in one of the hard places in the world, a place still unreached with the Good News, you will learn to expect angels to serve both you and those who will one day be saved. Angels play an important role in the battle between good and evil that rages in those places, and the intervention of angels just might convince someone to follow Jesus.

Going Further: Recommended Reading
McKnight, Scot. *The Hum of Angels: Listening for the Messengers of God Around Us.* New York, NY: Waterbrook, 2017.
Orthner, Jerry. *Angels: Friends in High Places.* Carmel, NY: Guideposts, 1997.

A Troubling Question: What About People Who Have Never Heard About Jesus?

CHAPTER SEVEN

Natasha's Story

In 1995, Russia was recovering from seventy years under communist rule. Communism was being dismantled, and people were tasting freedom in ways they had never experienced it before.

I met Natasha on my first visit to a newly established Christian church. She had just graduated from university with a degree in English language and literature. I asked her to help me learn Russian. She became much more than a language helper—we became good friends.

Is There a God?

When I met Natasha in 1995, she was a new believer in Jesus. Her story raised for me a very difficult question that still troubles me to this day—I can't forget it.

Natasha grew up in Russia during the harshness of the Soviet regime. During this time, the church had been driven underground, perhaps even more deeply out of sight than I experienced in Romania during the eighties. She never once heard the name of Jesus, not even as a curse word, until near the end of her university years. Neither had she ever heard about this thing we call "church."

Natasha's childhood education took place in a Marxist system shaped by "scientific atheism."* Her elementary school years were marked by the ruthless indoctrination* for which communist educators were famous. Natasha had an inquiring mind, which often got her into trouble at school. She seemed to always be asking the wrong questions. She never found it easy to accept uncritically the things her teachers taught her.

One day on her way to school, she was suddenly overwhelmed by the beauty of nature around her. Southern Russia is such a beautiful place. At school she had been taught that all of creation was the result of chance,[62] but as she walked to school that day, an observation popped uninvited into her mind: "All this beauty in nature around me couldn't have just *happened*, as the teacher tells us." And that thought triggered another: "There must at least be some Power, *someone* or something that triggered the evolutionary process."

As she walked along, a voice whispered a dangerous answer to the questions swirling inside her head: "Such beauty didn't just happen. Maybe there is a God!"

There is No God

When she arrived at school, young Natasha couldn't contain herself. Not knowing any better, she blurted out to the teacher, "Is there a God?"

The teacher's face instantly filled with shock and fear. "You must never ask such a question, child," she quickly replied.

But Natasha's naiveté pushed her to expand on the question: "But, Respected Teacher, the forests were so beautiful this morning! Did God make them?"

Her teacher flew into a rage and announced that Natasha would remain after class to write lines, punishment for such an outrageous and unscientific question.

After her classmates had left that afternoon, Natasha stood at the chalkboard, tears running down her cheeks as she wrote "There is no God!" one thousand times.

Several days later, she walked home from school, noticing that the leaves were now turning a brilliant gold and red as winter approached. Natasha was once again overcome with a naive sense that Someone must have created the beautiful forests along the pathway that led to her home.

I know it couldn't have just happened! she told herself. *But how?* She couldn't help but remember the line she had written one thousand times on the chalkboard: There is no God!

Arriving home to the dark little apartment where she lived with her family, she felt as though the dangerous thoughts tumbling around in her head would make it explode. She was overcome by an inexplicable sense of *something* she couldn't explain.

Not understanding what was happening, Natasha fell to her knees in the living room, lifted her hands above her head, and cried loudly, "O God, if there is a God, please show me who you are!"

---

62   In every textbook, whether for science, history, math, or English language, the left page of the open textbook would present the cold, hard facts. On the facing page the communist interpretation of the facts would be explained through the lenses of scientific atheism and communist ideology.

Ten years passed, and Natasha graduated from high school and entered the Kuban State University of Krasnodar. This was during the era of *perestroika*.[63] As the communist regime began to fall apart, people were experiencing freedom of thought and religion for the first time. It was a period of unprecedented openness to new ideas.

Natasha loved learning and had many friends, among them foreigners, who for the first time in seventy years had been able to get visas to travel to Russia. Foreigners flooded the universities in her city, telling everyone about Jesus.

One day, a friend invited her to a Bible study. Nowhere in her program of English language and literature had Natasha ever heard about the book her friend mentioned, the Bible. Intrigued, she went with her friend to an English study group that was discussing this unknown book. In the very first study, she heard the answer to her childhood question, "Is there a God?" She learned that there *is* a God—and what's more, God has a Son whose name is Jesus. God loved her so much he sent his Son Jesus to earth, to die and pay the penalty for her sins. Almost immediately Natasha opened her heart to Jesus and became a committed follower.

A Very Troubling Question

When I heard her story, it raised a troubling question in my mind. I couldn't get rid of the image of a young girl on her knees in the dark living room of her family home, hands raised above her head, speaking to someone that her teacher said didn't exist.

The words she cried out that day, "O God, if there is a God, please show me who you are!" haunted me. What if Natasha hadn't lived long enough to hear about Jesus? What if, for some reason, Natasha had died the night she cried out to God, never having heard of Jesus, never knowing the answer to her question?

I wondered where she would have gone after she died. I certainly believed in heaven. I didn't want to believe in hell, but I did. Everywhere I went in those days in Russia—a country finally wide open to the Good News about Jesus—I met young Russians, all of whom had grown up during the Soviet era, and most of whom had never heard of Jesus. What is the eternal future of the many people in the world today who still have never heard about Jesus?

---

63 *Perestroika* (meaning "restructuring") was a political movement of reformation within the Communist Party in the Soviet Union during the late 1980s and 90s. It is widely associated with the Soviet leader Mikhail Gorbachev and his *glasnost* ("openness") policy reform. He introduced a series of political and economic reforms that he thought would kickstart the stagnant economy of the Soviet Union. Instead, his reforms led to the disintegration of communism as it had been known in the Soviet Union during the seventy years since the Russian Revolution.

Two years later I was back in Canada, speaking in every church that would invite me. Every chance I got, I told Natasha's story, ending with the little girl kneeling in her dingy living room in southern Russia, hands raised, crying out, "O God, if there is a God, please show me who you are."

I would invite listeners to help me think about the question that was troubling me: If Natasha had died that night, would she have gone to heaven? It always started good discussions about whether people who have never heard about Jesus are lost. It was, and still is, a complex question that raises lots of other related questions.

Time to Reflect

1. Does the question this story raises bother you at all? Why? How should we think about this question as we think about taking the Good News to hard places today?
2. What do you already know and believe about this very complex missional issue?
3. Where can we go to explore the issue more deeply? Theologians and missiologists through the centuries have debated whether people who have never heard about Jesus are lost. The next section will take you to the Scriptures and the discipline of theology to think about the question.

Going Deeper

What does it mean to be lost? I remember once getting separated from my hiking buddies in the mountains. I was totally disoriented (hey, I'm directionally challenged), and didn't know whether to go right or left when I came to a fork in the path.

I was filled with panic because night was falling. I figured if I could find and follow the river, I'd eventually find a road and some people. But which way was the river? I knew the sun sets in the west, but it was so overcast I couldn't see where the sun was setting. I was far away from anyone who could show me the way. I knew I was lost, and it was a terrifying feeling.

Are People Who Have Never Heard About Jesus Lost?
When I ask if people who have never heard about Jesus are "lost," I'm asking if they're separated from God. Or are they saved? The question raises many others: If they aren't followers of Jesus, will they spend eternity apart from God when they die?

Statistics tell us that there are 7.8 billion people in the world (as of 2020), and only 2.2 billion call themselves *Christian*.[64] That means that only one third of all the people in the world have some understanding of who Jesus is. And at least one third of all the people in the world don't have easy access to knowing Jesus because there is no one near who can tell them. They live in a place, culture, or language group without any evangelizing church. Unless someone goes into that group from the outside, these people have no way of knowing about Jesus. When we who care about lost people refer to groups who've never heard about Jesus, we call them Unreached People Groups (UPGs for short).[65]

Is knowing about or even just acknowledging there is a God enough to save a person from judgment when they die? The question I'm really asking is: what does a person have to know in order to be saved?

How Much Does a Person Have to Know to be Saved?

Natasha was moved toward belief in God's existence by looking at nature. The Apostle Paul believed that through creation God's existence and his power are clearly revealed to everyone. In Romans he writes that the basic reality of God is pretty plain. *"Open your eyes and there it is!"* Paul says. *"By taking a long and thoughtful look at what God has created, people have always been able to see what their eyes as such can't see: eternal power, for instance, and the mystery of his divine being. So nobody has a good excuse"* (Romans 1:19–20, MSG).

---

64 The label "Christian" can be confusing. People who call themselves Christians may be Christian in name only—perhaps church attendees or people who simply hold to some form of cultural or denominational Christianity without understanding who Jesus is. Most sources suggest that roughly 31% of the world is "Christian."

65 A. Scott Moreau, Gary R. Corwin, and Gary B. McGee, *Introducing World Missions: A Biblical, Historical, and Practical Survey*, 2nd edition (Grand Rapids, MI: Baker Academic, 2015), p. 18. An Unreached People Group is a group that currently has little access to the gospel. They are *hidden*—not that they are invisible, but in the sense that there is no way under current conditions that they can hear the gospel in their own language in a way that makes sense to them. According to the Joshua Project (https://joshuaproject.net/), an Unreached People Group doesn't have enough followers of Jesus or the resources needed to evangelize their own people, so they need help from the outside to do so.

The question is whether what is revealed about God through nature (theologians call that *general* revelation)*[66] is enough to save a person from spiritual death and eternal judgement. Romans 2:14–16 goes even further by saying that the requirements of God's law are written in the heart of every person. Each one's innate moral judgment or conscience tells them what God requires of them. Paul says,

> *When outsiders who have never heard of God's law follow it more or less by instinct, they confirm its truth by their obedience. They show that God's law is not something alien, imposed on us from without, but woven into the very fabric of our creation. There is something deep within them that echoes God's yes and no, right and wrong. Their response to God's yes and no will become public knowledge on the day God makes his final decision about every man and woman.* (MSG)

Paul continues in this passage to suggest that just as Jews cannot be saved by keeping the Jewish law, neither are Gentiles saved by the general knowledge they get about God from creation. Using circumcision as the example, Paul says to Jews—who put great stock in having been circumcised,[67] proving they have kept all the Jewish laws—that all people live under the power of sin:

> *Circumcision, the surgical ritual that marks you as a Jew, is great if you live in accord with God's law. But if you don't, it's worse than not being circumcised. The reverse is also true. The uncircumcised who keep God's ways are as good as the circumcised—in fact, better. Better to keep God's law uncircumcised than break it [while] circumcised. Don't you see: it's not the cut of a knife that makes you a Jew. You become a Jew by who you* are. *It's the mark of God on your heart, not of a knife on your skin, that makes you a Jew. And recognition comes from God, not legalistic critics.*
> —Romans 2:25–29, MSG (emphasis in original)

---

66 Theologians speak of *general* and *special* revelation. General revelation refers to general truths that can be known about God as revealed through nature. Special revelation is how God has chosen to reveal himself through miraculous means, the ultimate form of special revelation being the person of Jesus Christ, whom John the Apostle calls the Word, God revealed in flesh (John 1:14). Another form of special revelation by God of primary importance is his Word, the Bible. Special revelation also includes dreams, visions, and physical appearances of God.

67 The special meaning of circumcision for the people of Israel is found in Genesis 17; it was imposed on Abraham and his descendants as a token of covenant membership in God's family.

Paul's final conclusion is that all human beings, Jew and Gentile, are lost. No one is righteous—not one of us. No one seems to understand the truth. He says so clearly: *"… doing what the law prescribes will not make anyone right in the eyes of God…"* (Romans 3:20, VOICE). *"You see, all have sinned, and all their futile attempts to reach God in His glory fail… they are now saved and set free by His free gift of grace through the redemption available only in Jesus the Anointed"* (Romans 3:23–24, VOICE).

When I think about Natasha, I draw hope from the reality that if someone responds obediently to what God reveals of himself in nature, God will send more light—often through a human messenger. That's pretty special. In fact, the revelation brought by the messenger is what we call *special* revelation,* which includes everything God has revealed about himself through Christ and the Scriptures. Of course, the supreme Messenger or special revelation of God was his Son, Jesus, who came as a human being to show us who God is. That's why John 3:16–17 says:

This is how much God loved the world: He gave his Son, his one and only Son. And this is why: so that no one need be destroyed; by believing in him, anyone can have a whole and lasting life. God didn't go to all the trouble of sending his Son merely to point an accusing finger, telling the world how bad it was. He came to help, to put the world right again. Anyone who trusts in him is acquitted; anyone who refuses to trust him has long since been under the death sentence without knowing it. And why? Because of that person's failure to believe in the one-of-a-kind Son of God when introduced to him. (MSG)

Do People Have to Know About Jesus?

It seems that what God shows of himself in nature isn't what saves someone from the death sentence mentioned in these verses. People have to know about Jesus. John says that by believing in him, anyone can have *"a whole and lasting life."* God sent Jesus to reveal his love. It's quite comforting to me that God sent an American who was enthusiastic about the gospel to students at Kuban State University of Krasnodar. She was a human messenger who could explain who Jesus is to people like Natasha who were lost. She, and others like her, introduced students to the Bible, which clearly reveals to its readers who Jesus is. No wonder theologians give the name "special revelation" to the message Jesus brought when he came to earth—and also to God's Word, the Bible.

If seeing God in creation isn't enough, what do people need to know and understand about God in order to be saved from eternal death? They must know that

God has a son. Simply put, people must know about Jesus. The solution to the terrible, lost condition of people who have never heard about Jesus is a person who is sent by God—a person that Paul says has "beautiful feet," because she goes to tell lost people about Jesus. Paul says,

> *How, then, can they call on the one they have not believed in? And how can they believe in the one of whom they have not heard? And how can they hear without someone preaching to them? And how can they preach unless they are sent? As it is written, "How beautiful are the feet of those who bring good news!"*
> —Romans 10:14–15

Is Jesus the Only Way?

There is another question that we have to think about that has to do with the uniqueness of Jesus: "Is Jesus the only way?" A friend of mine thinks some Christians are very narrow-minded, especially those who believe that salvation is found only in Jesus. She isn't happy that people like me think that believing in God (or a god) isn't enough.

My response to this friend is that truth is narrow. We don't consider it to be mathematical prejudice or narrow-mindedness to claim that four plus four equals eight rather than ten or twelve or twenty. It's a matter of truth. That is why Jesus said, *"I am the way and the truth and the life. No one comes to the Father except through me"* (John 14:6). These are his own words. So, whether it seems narrow or not, Jesus is clearly the only way to God. Truth is narrow.

That's Not Fair!

One Sunday night, I told Natasha's story to a youth group in a church in southern Alberta. The junior high youth joined the high school group that night to hear me speak. The younger teens were restless, and I'm quite sure they didn't hear very much of what the missionary was saying. However, the promise of pizza after the Bible study motivated them to sit reasonably quietly for thirty minutes. One of the youngest—about thirteen years old, sitting in the front row with a baseball cap pulled down over his eyes—squirmed uncomfortably the whole time. He was right in front of me, but I was pretty sure he didn't hear or understand a word I said, much less care about it.

I finished Natasha's story with the usual provocative question: "Here is my question for you guys! If Natasha had died that night, after she called out to God to reveal himself to her, where would she have spent eternity?" I asked the students to discuss the question in small groups and report back to the group in fifteen minutes, with Scripture to support their answer.

When the students gathered to report back to the large group, we heard different perspectives on the fate of Natasha, who had never heard about Jesus at the time she cried out to God. They even raised some new questions that had come up—was she saved? Unsaved? Do only saved people go to heaven? As I always am, they were as troubled that through no fault of her own, Natasha had never heard about Jesus.

Some students used Romans 10:13, *"Everyone who calls on the name of the Lord will be saved,"* to consider Natasha's destiny had she died. They suggested that because she had never called on Jesus, the Lord, to save her, she wouldn't have gone to heaven. Others believed she would have gone to heaven because she was responding to the light of nature that God had shown her. They argued that in a sense, she *had* called on the Lord. Another group was quite sure that because God is good and knows every heart, he wouldn't have condemned a sincere seeker like Natasha to hell.

As the discussion wound down, I admitted it was still a very difficult and troubling question for me. The pastor sitting in the back row cringed when I grinned and suggested they be sure to ask him how he would answer the question. It's a difficult one!

Three Views on Those Who Have Never Heard About Jesus

Traditionally there have been three approaches to answering this difficult question. One view, which people call the "exclusivist view," states without apology that Jesus is the only Saviour of the world. Those who hold this view say that to be saved, a person must believe in God's special revelation of himself in the life, death, and resurrection of Jesus. That's pretty exclusive!

In contrast, the "inclusivist view" agrees that Jesus is the only Saviour of the world, but argues that a person doesn't have to hear the gospel[68] to be saved. In other words, if anyone *is* saved, it is because of the death of Jesus. Not everyone will hear the gospel, but those who respond in faith to the revelation they *do* have will be saved. Inclusivists believe that salvation is only in Christ, but that knowledge of Christ's work is not necessary for salvation. John Sanders, who is an inclusivist, says "people might receive the gift of salvation without knowing the giver or the precise nature of the gift."[69]

---

68 There are many good definitions of the gospel. For simplicity I give one from Scripture: *"... that Christ died for our sins according to the Scriptures, that he was buried, that he was raised on the third day according to the Scriptures..."* (1 Corinthians 15:3–4).

69 John Sanders, *No Other Name: An Investigation into the Destiny of the Unevangelized* (Grand Rapids, MI: Eerdmans, 1992), p. 216.

A third view, called "pluralism," says that all paths are valid and all lead to God. This view opens the door to believing that people who faithfully follow world religions other than Christianity can be saved.[70]

Because I always stick close to Scripture when trying to answer such questions,[71] my head has always led me toward the exclusivist view (see below). But in today's culture, some people say that "exclusivism" is culturally insensitive, narrow-minded, intolerant, and dogmatic—all being words the culture around us doesn't want to hear. When I discuss this complex issue with people, I often feel like I lose my audience before they even engage with me because my answer sounds rather "exclusive." I keep referring them back to God's Word, the Scriptures, on the subject.

> The biggest question for me is whether there is any basis to hope that those who don't hear about Jesus in this life will be saved.

The issue raises so many troubling questions. The biggest question for me is whether there is any basis to hope that those who don't hear about Jesus in this life will be saved. There are at least nine different ways in which people who call themselves Christians have answered that question. These responses fall along a spectrum: at one end of the continuum is the position that people must hear the gospel and trust Christ to be saved.[72] At the other end is pluralism, holding that all major religions are equally valid, and Christ and Christianity aren't unique.[73]

Is There any Basis to Hope that Those Who Don't Hear About Jesus in this Life Will Be Saved?

As I talked with the teenagers that night, I explained that my answer to the question heading this paragraph is "No." That means I hold to the exclusivist view. I believe that, with the coming of Jesus Christ, the focus of faith was narrowed to one man. He was the fulfillment of all the sacrifices and prophecies in the Old Testament. Whether a person lived before Jesus' death or after, all saving faith points in trust to what Jesus did for us on the Cross. Our faith looks to his death to atone for the sins of all time.

A Story from Acts 4

I told the group a story from Acts 4 that is helpful in determining what one must know to be saved. Peter and John healed a beggar known to everyone, which raised

---

71   The Scripture is God's authoritative Word. I hold as belief only that which agrees with what God has revealed in his Word, the Bible.

a lot of suspicion among religious leaders. That gave Peter an opportunity to preach a fine message to the Jewish crowd, telling them that it was by the name of Jesus Christ that he and John had healed the crippled man the day before.

As Peter preached, he clearly told the crowd the story of Jesus' death and resurrection. He announced the Good News that Jesus had died to forgive the sins of each one of them, but he made it clear that they had to repent and believe (Acts 3:19). Over and over, Peter and John referred to the power of Jesus' name. They spoke of having faith in that name (verse 16). Imagine, five thousand people came to believe in Jesus that day!

Even though Peter and John spent that night in prison because of their message, they continued the next day to speak about Jesus, who had died and risen from the dead just a few months earlier. Peter again told the crowd that there was something about the very name of Jesus that would bring about salvation for anyone who believed in his name. Referring to Jesus, Peter told them, *"Salvation is found in* no one *else, for there is no other name under heaven given to [people] by which we must be saved"* (Acts 4:12, emphasis added).

Peter had just told thousands of religiously-minded listeners the story of Jesus. He reminded them of their Jewish history, and explained that in Jesus Christ all of salvation history was narrowed down to one Person. He was pointing their thoughts to Jesus when he said very clearly that salvation could be *"found in no one else."* If I were to say that a person can be saved without believing in Jesus, it would mean that Jesus didn't really need to die after all. It would suggest that there was some other way. It would make a mockery of Jesus' death.

With the youth that evening, I reminded them that during Natasha's childhood, she had never ever heard the name of Jesus—not once! Through the beauty of creation (general revelation), the existence and even the power of God had become crystal clear to her. Creation had prompted her to think about God, and it had prompted her to cry out to God to reveal himself to her. But it's hard to ignore the decisive words Peter used to finish his message, the words in Acts 4:12: *"Salvation is found in no one else, for there is no other name under heaven given to [people] by which we must be saved."*

That's Not Fair!

I looked out over the students sitting in front of me and said, "At that time in her life, Natasha hadn't yet believed in Jesus—how could she? She'd never heard about him. So, she wasn't saved. If I take direction from Acts 4:12, Natasha wouldn't have gone to heaven because she wasn't saved, and as I understand heaven, it's only for saved people. To be saved, you must believe in Jesus."

The room fell quiet.

Suddenly, the young boy in the front row—who I'd assumed hadn't been listening to a word I'd said all evening—rose to his feet, pulled his baseball cap off his head, and yelled in a very loud and angry voice, "That's not fair!" He sat down and lowered his head into his hands.

The room became instantly quiet. All eyes were on me. Into the silence I said three short sentences: "You're right! It's not fair! *That* is why I'm a missionary!"

There Must Be a Gospel Messenger

My exclusivist view, rooted in Scripture, leads me to say that salvation is found only in the work of Jesus. I believe that God uses general revelation (God revealed in creation) as one step in the process toward salvation—it often serves as a preparation for the gospel.[74] A person might see God in creation, but there must still be a gospel messenger who points them to God's son, Jesus, who died for them. I say that because I believe that the gospel is the only means of salvation. For that reason, I call myself a "gospel exclusivist."[75]

This is why the church must focus its best efforts on evangelism and missions. God's "ordinary" way of bringing people to faith in Jesus is by sending the gospel, usually carried by a messenger, to those who have never heard of him. Seeing God in creation isn't enough. That's why I'm an international worker!

There are some "exclusivists" who believe, as I do, that the church should focus on sending messengers. They also recognize, as I do, that God might choose to send a special revelation to someone who has never heard the Good News using an "extraordinary" means. If you remember my stories in the last chapter, God often works in supernatural ways. The Holy Spirit might choose to use a direct revelation from God: a dream,[76] a vision, a miracle, or an angel bringing a gospel message to someone who has never heard the Good News.

---

74 John Piper, *Let the Nations Be Glad! The Supremacy of God in Missions* (Grand Rapids, MI: Baker, 1993), p. 151–159.

75 I am using the label developed in Morgan and Peterson's book, *Faith Comes by Hearing*, p. 26–28. Borland, whom Morgan and Peterson quote, suggests that according to this position a person must hear the gospel and trust Christ to be saved.

76 As a small child, the gospel was ultimately clarified to me by a dream in which I also heard the voice of God. How could I not believe that sometimes God uses "extraordinary" means to bring people to faith?

I remind myself every day that the customary way by which sinners come to know and love God is through a messenger bringing the Good News of what Jesus did in dying for them. So, when I pray for Unreached People Groups, I always pray that God will raise up many in the next generation who will go as messengers. But I'm glad that sometimes God uses extraordinary ways to bring the message of Jesus to lost people.[77]

Is it Just for God to Send People Who Have Never Heard the Gospel to Hell?

As I work through the spectrum of nine different responses to the sobering question, "Is there any basis for hope that those who don't hear about Jesus in this life will be saved?" I see some responders trying, optimistically, to find a hope of salvation apart from the gospel. They ask the sincere question, "Is it just or fair for God to send people to hell who have never heard the gospel?" They want to widen the doorway of hope to include other ways to salvation.

Inclusivists, which is what we call such people, charge exclusivists like me with unfairness and injustice. Like the young boy in the youth group, they cry out, "It's not fair!" How could it be fair and just for those who have not heard the gospel, which is necessary for salvation, to be lost forever? But behind their accusation that "It's not fair!" are two faulty assumptions.[78]

> How could it be fair and just for those who have not heard the gospel, which is necessary for salvation, to be lost forever?

1) Condemned Because We Are Sinners

The first mistaken assumption is that people are condemned because they have rejected the gospel. But remember that the people we're talking about haven't even heard the gospel, so they haven't rejected it. The Bible is completely clear that condemnation isn't based on rejecting the gospel but on the fact that we are sinners.

Romans 5:18 says, *"So here is the result: one man's sin [Adam] brought condemnation and punishment for all people"* (VOICE, emphasis in original). Paul also says that God's wrath is revealed against anyone (Jew or Gentile alike) who rejects God's truth as revealed through creation (Romans 1:18–25). In Romans, Paul argues that

---

77 People who believe God sometimes uses special revelations of himself beyond Christ and the Scriptures might be called "special revelation exclusivists." See Morgan and Peterson, *Faith Comes by Hearing*, p. 28–29 for a more complete explanation.

78 Morgan and Peterson (p. 241–243) again give an excellent, succinct response to the question, "Is it just for God to send people to hell who have never heard of Jesus?" My discussion is based on theirs.

just as everyone has innate knowledge of God, rebellion is also innate. Rebellion is the basis of our guilt.[79]

Natasha's condemnation was because she was a sinner, not because she had rejected (or had never heard) the gospel. Natasha cried out to God. She wasn't rebelling against him, but she was still guilty before him. Whenever I thought about that, as I pondered the fairness of God against which the young boy protested, I took hope for people like Natasha who turn to God and cry out based on the light of general revelation.

Natasha needed Jesus to save her from sin. God could have used extraordinary means (a dream or vision or an angelic messenger) to communicate the gospel. But freedom to evangelize came to Russia, and with freedom came a human messenger who told her about Jesus.

2) A Confusion of Justice and Mercy

The second mistaken assumption behind the assertion of unfairness is our tendency to confuse justice and mercy. Yes, it *is* just and fair for God to punish those who are guilty because they are sinners.[80] God wasn't obliged to provide salvation for guilty sinners, but it is merciful and gracious that he did so. As Morgan and Peterson say, "…because of his grace and mercy (in a way consistent with his justice), God made atonement for our sins through Christ's death and resurrection. And in grace and mercy, God sends good news to the guilty so they can repent and trust Christ."[81]

The question, "Is it fair that God punishes those who have never heard the gospel?" must be answered with a "yes." We continue by asking, "Is it fair that millions will never hear the gospel?" My stomach writhes as I respond, "No it is not." *That* was actually the issue against which the young boy in the youth group protested. He was angry because without a messenger Natasha was lost, as are millions today. I don't question the justice of God's punishment of the guilty, but I am troubled that the news of God's mercy has reached so few. It isn't fair!

---

79 William Edgar writes a chapter in Morgan and Peterson's book called "Exclusivism: Unjust or Just?," p. 78–97.

80 Morgan and Peterson, *Faith Comes by Hearing*, p. 242.

81 Ibid.

All of us stand condemned before a holy God, deserving his anger. In that, God is fair. Perhaps there is greater condemnation for those of us who live in Christianized, developed countries with centuries of Christian history and access to the Bible. We bear more condemnation than those in places where the reach of the gospel is limited. Why? Because we know about Jesus but keep that Good News to ourselves.

All of us stand condemned before a holy God, deserving his anger. In that, God is fair. Perhaps there is greater condemnation for those of us who live in Christianized, developed countries with centuries of Christian history and access to the Bible.

Perhaps We Are the Problem

The greatest mystery to me isn't the character of God (his love, his justice, or his mercy) or the destiny of lost people. The greatest mystery is why we, who have God's Word and could share the story of Jesus with people who are lost, don't go to those who haven't heard.

Robertson McQuilkin, who went to Japan to tell lost Japanese people about Jesus, asks why we who know Jesus are busy doing other things—maybe even very good things—but aren't going ourselves, or sending others, until every single person now alive has heard about Jesus.[82] The problem isn't with God's character but with our obedience to the last command of Jesus, *"Therefore go and make disciples of all nations, baptizing them in the name of the Father and of the Son and of the Holy Spirit"* (Matthew 28:19).

Going Further: Recommended Reading

McQuilkin, Robertson. *The Great Omission: A Biblical Basis for World Evangelism.* Waynesboro, GA: Authentic Media, 2002.

Morgan, Christopher W., and Robert A. Peterson, eds. *Faith Comes by Hearing: A Response to Inclusivism.* Downers Grove, IL: IVP Academic, 2008.

---

82 Robertson McQuilkin, *The Great Omission: A Biblical Basis for World Evangelism* (Waynesboro, GA: Authentic Media, 2002), p. 52.

Serving Solo: Singleness in Mission

CHAPTER EIGHT

Is it Okay to Be Single?

I sit and wait. One by one, the women arrive for our evening meeting. Without a word, they enter the little apartment where we meet in secret. They hug tightly as they greet each other softly with *"Pace!"*—"Peace!" They take seats on chairs and beds that line the walls of the room. Some have been waiting for several hours already—they arrive separately so as not to attract the attention of neighbours or be noticed by the secret police who often hang around in the street below. It is important that no one suspect that something "unauthorized" is happening in Teo and Sanda's apartment on the third floor.

After teaching and learning is finished for the day, Pastor Teo sits with me to explain the schedule he has planned for tomorrow. With his limited English, learned from many contacts with Westerners, Teo explains that the next morning I will meet with the "girls." He uses the English word *girls* to translate the Romanian word *fete*, which refers to unmarried women, particularly those who have never had a child. He continues, "And in the afternoon you will meet with the women," translating the Romanian word *femei*, which means married women, especially those who have children.

His distinction between *girls* and *women* feels intentional, as is his division of the students into two distinct groups. I am thirty-five years old now. Hurt pride rises inside me as I hear half of the students referred to as girls. I, too, am a girl (*fată*) by their definition, because I'm unmarried and have never had a child. I want to fight back!

Looking Teo in the eyes, I ask—hoping he hears in my voice a slight tone of jest—"So will I always be a *girl* just because I'm not married?"

With a reciprocal hint of a grin in his eyes, Teo responds. I can see he is carefully choosing his words, realizing that his response might offend me. But he trusts the warm friendship I've built with him and his wife. "No, Miriam, in our language you are an *old girl (fată bătrână)*."[83]

The meaning is very clear! In their culture, though I am only in my thirties, I am an "old maid," a "spinster," because I'm unmarried and have never borne a child. I hate those words. I recognize the hurt feelings rising within. I know I have to deal with my less-than-sanctified emotional reaction!

Time to Reflect

1. Does this story raise in your mind an issue that you think people who will go to a hard place on mission should think about? Have you thought about it before? Are there questions you think deserve to be discussed?
2. What do you already know about the issue?
3. Where can we go to explore the issue more deeply? Theologians and mission historians have written about singleness and mission, especially the contribution of single women in the history of mission. The next part of the chapter will help you think about the issue of singleness with the disciplines of theology and mission history as the lenses.

Going Deeper

Early the next morning, while it is still dark, someone drives me to a pig farm just outside the city limits. Pastor Teo says the Securitate would never suspect that Christians meet at such a place. For three hours I meet with twelve single women between the ages of twenty-two and twenty-nine. We are "girls" together for a morning. This label still makes me bristle with indignation every time I hear it applied to these women. They aren't *girls*! They are mature *women*, some of them holding positions of influence in the factories where they work. Is the label used to describe us purely a matter of language (there's no other word to translate *fete*), or is this really how Romanian Christians see us who aren't married?

For me, it's a perfect chance to unpack what I think the Bible says to people who aren't married, especially those who serve in the church. The women listen with open hearts. Never in their lives have they had a frank discussion about singleness and what it means to be single in the church.

---

83 Even today, Romanian audiences laugh when I tell this story. Those who understand English realize it is primarily a matter of unnuanced translation. Most realize how potentially hurtful the phrase is. Some want to console me, but most just enjoy the moment as much as I enjoy telling the story!

My thinking about singleness has been shaped by friendship with a wonderful single woman in Canada, Julie Fehr. Julie worked for thirty years as an international worker in the jungles of Gabon. She was a few years ahead of me in the journey. When I talked with her about singleness, her starting place was always the question, "What is the purpose of life?" I would ask myself what life purpose had to do with whether I was married or not. But I knew how Julie would answer the question. She would quote the Westminster Shorter Catechism,[84] which says that the chief purpose of human beings is to glorify God and then to enjoy him forever. It's not a phrase drawn directly from Scripture, but the truth about glorifying God is scattered through the Bible.

The Bible teaches that the primary purpose of Christians, and of everything and everyone God created, is to bring glory to him. There is no higher calling. It's one thing to say it, but I sometimes feel that it's hard to live out that purpose in a world so preoccupied with marriage, as though getting married is one of the primary purposes of life.

As the morning unfolds behind closed doors, a dozen single women share deeply with me on a topic they have never discussed before: what it's like to be unmarried in the church in Romania, or if married, to be childless.[85] How can singles bring glory to God when having children is a priority of the regime—and when getting married and having children is a major preoccupation in their church, too? Life seems to suggest it's not okay to be single! Everyone in the church wants to get the singles married off!

All my adult life, I've assumed I will get married. Canadian culture hasn't helped me to see God's glory in singleness. The media is filled with images of couples. Married people often speak of their spouse as their "better half." The women with me this morning tell me that there are equivalent expressions in Romanian.

Sometimes when I hear the term "better half," I protest inwardly. I refuse to believe that I'm only half a person until I find someone to complete me. But sometimes

---

84 *The Westminster Shorter Catechism* asks the question, "What is the chief end of man?" This catechism is among the most rich and concise summaries of Christian beliefs ever written. Compiled for the Westminster Assembly in 1647 and finalized in 1648, the *Shorter Catechism* was originally designed as a method of instructing children and new converts in the Christian faith. It is now in the public domain.

85 Childless couples and single people without children were penalized financially by the state each month due to President Ceausescu's determination to raise the population of Romania from 23 to 30 million by the year 2000. For that reason, childlessness was a stigma in society. The church idealized marriage, so singleness was stigmatized there as well.

I still find myself longing to finally meet that person. This morning I read Romans 12:1–2 with the women:

> … I urge you, [sisters], in view of God's mercy, to offer your bodies as living sacrifices, holy and pleasing to God—this is your true and proper worship. Do not conform to the pattern of this world, but be transformed by the renewing of your mind. Then you will be able to test and approve what God's will is—his good, pleasing and perfect will.

We wonder together if we have allowed the subtle pressures from the world around us, or maybe even expectations from within the church, to stifle God's glory from shining from our lives. We stop and together ask God to give us the transformed mind Paul speaks about—so that whether married or single we will be able to clearly discern God's purpose for our life. We ask him to help us see ourselves as *whole* persons bringing glory to God.

In some cultures where you will serve, being single might be a big concern for the people you live among. There seems to be an almost universal reaction to singleness—people want to see you married! Without realizing it, people are reflecting God's words to the first human being, *"It is not good for [humans] to be alone. I will make a helper…"* (Genesis 2:18). I've reminded God of those words so many times. My niece once announced to me that she wanted to be single like me because she saw how fulfilled I am, but I quickly reminded her that marriage, generally speaking, is God's plan. God knew what he was talking about when he said it isn't good to be alone. Even God thrives in community—his life in the Trinity, the Father's indivisible oneness with the Holy Spirit and the Son, his intimate "three in one" existence, points to the reality that God lives in community.

Very soon after God first declared, "It is not good to be alone," he instituted marriage. That makes me think, generally speaking, that marriage is what God planned.

A Three-Dimensional Person

On the farm on the outskirts of Oradea that morning, I read 1 Thessalonians 5:23 with twelve unmarried women.

> Now, may the God of peace and harmony set you apart, making you completely holy. And may your entire being—spirit, soul, and body—be kept completely flawless in the appearing of our Lord Jesus, the Anointed One. The one who calls you by name is trustworthy and will thoroughly complete his work in you.
> —1 Thessalonians 5:23–24, TPT

Julie Fehr's very practical teaching on these verses had impacted me several years earlier, as she and I wrestled together with the reality of living as single women in a world that prioritizes marriage. Those discussions and her writing[86] had left an indelible mark on me. At that time, Julie understood human personhood as three dimensional: spirit, soul, and body. Not three persons, but three aspects which together are a *whole* being.[87] Paul prays that each dimension will be made increasingly holy by God during our lifetime.

The Spiritual Dimension

Among the three dimensions of persons Paul names, he first names the spirit. What does it mean to be a *spiritual* being? My spirit is that part of me that communicates with God. Because God is Spirit, there are things in my life that I can only deal with at a spiritual level—his Spirit communicates with my spirit.

One of the subjects I've wrestled with in my spirit is the issue of wholeness. How often I have tried to achieve a sense of wholeness through relationships with people, hoping they will fill me up! At times it's pretty disappointing, because relationships sometimes leave me empty. In my early years, I found myself looking for a man who would make me whole, complete me in the places where I knew I was lacking. Maybe that's why I believed the lie that "opposites attract." I thought I'd find a man who had what I lacked, and together we would complete each other.

When I was in college, that thinking was challenged when I read Colossians 2:10, *"You, too, are being completed in Him…"* (VOICE). My completeness (wholeness) comes from Jesus. Wow! That excited me! The people around me, sometimes even people in the church, tried to convince me that if only I could find a man, I would finally be complete—whole.

What fun it is this morning to announce to the twelve *fete* (girls) sitting around me, all of them longing to be affirmed as *whole* people, that I can be completely

---

86 Julie Fehr, "Celebrating God: Being Single in a *Double* World," *The Alliance Witness* (February 13, 1985), p. 4–5, 11.

87 Julie Fehr died an untimely death in 1994 before the discussion among scholars about the dimensions of personhood arose. Today, thirty-five years later, scholars would debate whether the "spirit" and "soul" are quite as distinct as Julie's treatment suggests. For example, Jesus commands us to love God with all our heart, soul, mind, and strength (Mark 12:3), with no mention of "spirit." In recent years, writers such as Dallas Willard define "spirit," "heart" (in its biblical usage), and "will" as referring to the same entity. Thus, in Willard's understanding, "spirit" is distinguished from "soul," which he understands to be the mind and the spirit/will as a totality (Willard, *Renovation of the Heart: Putting on the Character of Christ* (Colorado Springs, CO: NavPress, 2002) p. 33–34). The book referred to here is Willard's best explanation of how the essential parts of the human person must change in the process of spiritual formation in Christ.

whole as a single person. We talk again about the fact that marriage doesn't complete anyone. I have friends who have shared their disappointment in their experience of marriage. They assumed they would find in their new husband what was missing in their life—perhaps where one was lacking, the other would fill the empty places. But very early into marriage, they realized that two incomplete people, both lacking wholeness in Christ, do not combine to create a *whole.*

Because we are human, broken, and so often "blow it," wholeness cannot be achieved through marriage. Colossians 2:10 says that *"We are completely filled with God as Christ's fullness overflows within us"* (TPT, emphasis in original). Only as we are *"filled with God"* can we experience wonderful wholeness in him.

Suddenly I feel sorry for the man God might bring into my less-than-whole life, a man whom I expect to do for me what I haven't allowed Jesus Christ to do— make me whole!

Identity in Christ

The discussion this morning, flowing from the verses in 1 Thessalonians 5, turns to the believer's identity in Christ. It's a wholeness that flows and grows from identifying with Jesus Christ, a spiritual awareness that happens by faith. It's a spiritual reality that impacts every part of life.[88]

We pray together, inviting God's Spirit to help us understand who we really are because of our relationship with Jesus. We ask God to make us *whole,* to show us how to live a life so full of Jesus that we don't need anything or anyone other than him to be complete. We dream together about what wholeness might look like when two people who have both found satisfaction in Jesus come together in marriage, becoming one. Adding marriage to the mix will be the *icing on the cake.* It's a picture of wholeness that cannot be easily described in words.

We also dream about what wholeness would look like if God never brought a partner into our life. If our identity is in Jesus Christ, we aren't waiting for another human to make us complete. We are already complete in Christ. I can be single and whole.

---

88 One of the best recent books I have read on our identity in Christ is Dan Sneed's *The Power of a New Identity: Overcoming a Broken Self-Image* (Lancaster, UK: Sovereign World, 2012). His treatment of the believer's identity in Christ includes an excellent appendix (p. 185–189) on the topic which is well worth studying. He speaks in Chapter 3 (p. 51–53) to the confusion of identity and self-image in many minds. Identity is who I am when I receive Jesus, becoming a new creation whom God sees as "in Christ," a new person with a new identity. Identity is a fact, while self-image is how I see myself, a mental picture composed of the conclusions I have reached about myself. They are two very different things. I highly recommend his book.

I Am Soul

Some writers, when talking about the soulish part of a human being, speak of the soul as the aspect of a person that houses the emotional and intellectual side and the ability to choose—the will.

The Emotional/Feeling Side of Me

I always feel very single, very alone, when I travel by myself in communist Europe. That's a response of the human soul—an awareness, a feeling. A woman alone in a restaurant always finds it hard to get the attention of a waiter, and it's even more difficult to get served! When I'm alone, needing to flag a taxi, I feel as though I almost have to throw myself in front of the vehicle to get it to stop for me. I feel invisible.

On the other hand, I feel single but oh so loved every time a student or student's husband walks me back to my hotel at night after darkness has fallen. I remind myself that my unmarried status isn't necessarily the issue in these situations. Married women travelling alone need to be cared for as well. But it's because I am unmarried that I so often travel alone in the harsh, physically demanding context of Eastern Europe.

The first time I heard myself referred to as a "girl," even though I was now well into my thirties, I was hurt. The feelings that rose inside me when Pastor Teo called the unmarried women "girls" reminded me that I have a soul—I am an emotional being. I realize now that my overly sensitive, emotional response to Teo, who was trying so bravely to use his limited English, shows me just how *unwhole* I am. He called me a "girl"—it hit me in the deepest part of my soul, and it hurt!

The Thinking/Intellectual Side of Me

Julie often reminded me that the soulish part of me is more than just emotion. I also have a good mind that can wrestle with what I read and hear. I don't have to let hurt feelings rule. I don't have to pout.

Many times, I've read what the Apostle Paul says about singleness in 1 Corinthians 7, but I don't always like it. In verse 8 he effectively says, "If you can possibly remain single—do so!" (paraphrased). Paul thought singleness was a good way to live! I really don't want to hear that—nor do any of the women in the circle today. But we realize that we can do more than just emote and feel sorry for ourselves. We have good minds. We can use them and work hard to understand what the Scriptures mean. And then, with gentleness, we can help others understand where some interpretations of Scripture are problematic.

Paul was an itinerant missionary. For some reason he thought the problems of a single person were fewer than those of a married person. For my married friends back in Vienna, their husbands and children are very legitimate reasons why they can't travel for weeks at a time, as I do. I've observed people like Julie, who could disappear into the forests in Gabon for weeks at a time and serve without distraction—because no one was waiting at home for her. There were times when Julie would lie on her cot in the windowless hut prepared by her Gabonese hosts and overhear the men outside discussing with concern that she must be very lonely in bed.

Paul writes about how short life is (1 Corinthians 7:29–31). He suggests that because of this, choosing to cultivate a marriage may not be a wise priority. Building a good marriage takes a lot of time. In fact, Paul clearly suggests in verse 32 that marriage might even distract one from serving God. I'm quite sure that if I announce that idea to these women, it won't be well-received—and I'm sure it will be misunderstood by men in the churches from which they come. The idea of women serving in the church is still very new, so maybe that's not the place to start. But it's true! For some women, God's call to serve him in a specific way might rule out the possibility of marriage, because it would make building a strong marriage very difficult.

Pastor Teo has by now rejoined our Saturday morning discussion. He listens with traces of concern in his face, wondering where this conversation is leading. He points a finger at me and asks bluntly how much of each year I'm away from home. When I reply that I'm usually gone from home fifty to sixty percent of the year he responds, "Well, I'd find it hard to be married to you!"

The group laughs! I laugh as well, but my soul feels small and a little wounded, because I know it's true. We pray together that morning that God will give us minds that discern truth and then help us live in that truth in spite of hurt feelings.

The Choosing Side of Me: My Will
Another dimension of the "soulish" part of me, using Julie's understanding of human personality, is my will—that part of me that chooses (or refuses) to align my desires with God's. Having a will means I'm responsible for what I choose to make my focus in life. As I teach the women this morning, I feel such joy when I look around the circle. I realize what a privilege God has given me in allowing me to speak into the lives of the next generation. These women will, in turn, train the next generation, perhaps even helping those younger than them who are unmarried to recognize God's plan in their singleness.

This morning I whisper to myself, "Thank you, God, that I am single. I might not be here in Romania with these wonderful women if I were married!" I feel a deep sense of acceptance and fulfillment in this place where God has placed me. This morning, a phrase is birthed in me that I will share with many people in the years ahead: "I am a completely fulfilled, continually hopeful woman!"

In that phrase, two wonderful realities are meaningfully brought together: the rich fulfillment of doing ministry as a single woman, and the ongoing hope of one day being married. I'd like to be married, but when I dream of marriage, it's not as though I cannot be whole without that gift. I am living a full life. There is satisfaction in what I'm doing.

"I am a completely fulfilled, continually hopeful woman!"
In that phrase, two wonderful realities are meaningfully brought together: the rich fulfillment of doing ministry as a single woman, and the ongoing hope of one day being married.

And I am a fulfilled woman. Fulfillment seems to fit perfectly with the other reality—the hope that one day I will find a man who is also completely fulfilled in his calling to Jesus, and who hopes that God will bring a woman into his life who is completely fulfilled in her calling to Jesus.

The first reality (fulfillment) coexists with the second reality (hopefulness)— which for me remains a really important part of who I am as a woman. I never ask God to take that hopefulness from me. The longing for marriage remains, but the awareness of fulfillment helps me to live with the longing.

I Am Body

Our discussion this morning is rooted in Paul's prayer that our body, soul, and spirit will be kept flawless till Jesus comes. I am spirit, soul, and *body*. This aspect of my humanness, my physical body, is the most difficult one to talk about openly, maybe because I'm single.

So, usually I don't. I always find it difficult to openly admit that I am a virgin—that I have never had sex. But I sense this morning that sex is the very thing these women need to talk about. They hear me admit that I am very "alive," that I have God-given longings for sexual fulfillment which are a normal part of being human and being a woman. We don't apologize when we admit that we get hungry for food—sometimes even uncontrollably hungry. For some, enjoying food is an appetite that leads to bad choices! I remind them that in this discussion we *must* talk about the body, especially how to live with and manage the appetite for sex, which God created.

Just before Paul begins to write about marriage and singleness in 1 Corinthians 7, he writes quite simply, *"honor God with your bodies"* (1 Corinthians 6:20). This morning the women ask, a little shyly and with lots of relief, "Can we talk about how to honour God with our bodies? Remember that we aren't married. And our church tells us sex is for marriage—and yet the longing for sex is strong. We never talk about it!"[89]

I grew up believing that the only option for an unmarried person was to go through life unfulfilled—a half person, what Julie Fehr describes as "an emotional amputee with a wounded stump of self, exposed to all sorts of hurts."[90] I grew up believing that sex is for marriage, and I still believe it. I have friends who admit they chose to satisfy their physical longing for sex though they weren't married. On one occasion when I was in a relationship, I tested my conviction that sex is for marriage. I said "no" that day, though my body was screaming with desire.

For years, the alternatives seemed pathetic. How could I glorify God when abstinence didn't satisfy the raging of my body? But I believed it was the choice that honoured God. My struggling body was weak. I couldn't do this on my own. It's a very complex issue, not as cut-and-dried as some people think it is.

Fasting from Sex

Julie helped me think in a different way about my body, about sexual desire and singleness. She suggested I turn the voluntary or involuntary privation of intimacy and sexual fulfillment into a voluntary fast.[91] The truth is, usually there isn't a man (or woman) pressing me for sex. More often it's an involuntary privation. But the longing can still be intense. Julie suggested that by choosing to focus on my relationship with God instead of focusing on the intense longings of my body for intimacy, the lack of sexual involvement might be turned into a spiritual fast. I know it works

---

89 While the Bible doesn't talk specifically about sex outside of marriage, it repeatedly refers to "sexual immorality" or "sexual sins." These references are talking about *any* sexual activity outside of marriage, so they include having sex without being married. See 1 Corinthians 6:18–20; Colossians 3:5; 1 Thessalonians 4:3–4, 7; and Hebrews 13:4.

90 Fehr, "Celebrating God," p. 11.

91 Biblical fasting is abstaining from food for spiritual purposes. Going without food because it isn't available or for medical reasons is not biblical fasting. If a fast is biblical, there must be a spiritual motivation.

when I'm fasting from food. The awareness of gnawing hunger pangs somehow moves me toward an increasingly intimate connection with God.[92]

Julie told a story that helped me think about fasting from sexual desire. A small plane carrying two travellers crashed in northern Canada and wasn't discovered until thirty days later. When the wreckage was finally found, both travellers were dead—not from injuries or from exposure to the cold, but from starvation coupled with despair. Julie wondered if, had the travellers been Christians, they might have known about fasting. Instead of focusing on their lack of food and the hopelessness of the environment, they might have focused on God and survived, in spite of the involuntary privation of food.[93]

There were days in Romania when I didn't dare leave the train to look for food when it was stopped in a station. I was weak from hunger, and not because I had planned to fast (that would have been a voluntary privation). It was a lengthy, involuntary privation of food that I hadn't planned on. On these occasions, I turned the lack of food into a fast, an opportunity to heighten my desire for God above all other things or persons. My hunger took on purpose, and my relationship with God grew more personal and tangible. Somehow he felt very present to me in those moments of physical weakness. I wouldn't have traded that for food!

Could that also be true if the overwhelming longing for intimacy was turned into a fast? Could the privation of intimacy take on purpose in those moments?

One of the women asks me, very practically, "What do you *do* when you feel so *weak,* when the absence of intimacy is overwhelming and painfully real?" The question spawns a great discussion among the women. We speak about journaling, which is the way I sometimes find release from the painful reality of hunger. I couple it with prayer—and God draws near. I imagine his arms around me, and in my journal I write the expressions of intimacy that I hear him speak. One of the women shares that she finds the longing for intimacy often raises its head after long periods of inactivity—so she goes for a long walk or does something very physical, with ears open to

---

92 I could never understand when someone told me they were fasting but they had no time in their busy day to sit quietly with God and focus on relationship with him. For me, the essential motivation for fasting is taking time to grow my relationship with God, intentionally focusing on him while the body is raging with hunger and crying out for food, awakening a spiritual hunger for God, or demonstrating my love and desire for him above all else. When I fast and begin to feel hunger pangs, I experience the kindness of God's love and care for me, a deepening of my relationship of love with him. It is so beautiful. The intentional drawing near to God, not the abstaining from food, makes fasting most meaningful for me.

93 There are examples in Scripture, and many examples today, of human beings (Jesus being one of them) fasting for forty days and surviving.

his loving words. I deliberately choose to reach out to community when the longings are most real. I pour out my heart to a trusted friend who understands the fast, and responds with the reciprocal—not judgemental—affirmation that I am beloved.

How can I glorify God with my body when I cannot, voluntarily or involuntarily, satisfy the desires that are part of his creative design—this body that is sexually alive? Is it possible that my struggle with sexual desire and the cravings of my very "alive" body can become a pathway by which I can glorify God?

The idea of "celibacy,"[94] whether voluntary or involuntary, isn't an easy topic of discussion among people today. In fact, counsellors and therapists point people who are lonely, anxious, and broken toward intimacy—believing that the therapy of being "deeply known" is a powerful step toward healing.

We assume that living a celibate lifestyle means a deprivation of intimacy. We associate celibacy with sexual abstinence, as though that's the most important aspect of celibacy. But it's so much more than that. Thomas Aquinas spoke about celibacy as leaving space in our jam-packed lives for God, being free and available for his presence to invade us.[95]

Following Aquinas, Henri Nouwen describes celibacy as something for more than just clergy. He speaks of celibacy as creating and protecting a place of emptiness for God—creating or guarding some space in our lives into which we can invite God to come without being challenged. Nouwen suggests that this view of celibacy might be lived out in friendship, marriage, or singleness.[96] Extroverts like me, who love to serve and be with people, don't automatically make space for God in our "filled full" lives. It is an intentional, sometimes temporary, sometimes long-term practice, whether married or single, that keeps us from being dominated by our natural bodily impulses. It makes room for more of God's love, power, and grace, satisfying our deepest needs.

If my purpose in life is to glorify God, my body is part of the living sacrifice I offer to him (Romans 12:1–2). I offer him my spirit, soul, and body. My body is very much part of the living sacrifice (I read "living" as "aching, craving, yearning, and kicking") that I bring to God, a sacrifice that I know is pleasing to him.

This morning twelve single women, most of whom will marry in the years ahead, ask God to come into that place of emptiness they have intentionally created for him—a place where their deepest needs, including the need for intimacy, are met.

---

94 Abstaining from marriage and sexual relationships. In some church traditions, it is a lifetime vow; in other traditions, celibacy is a choice for a time.

95 Henri J. M. Nouwen, *Clowning in Rome* (New York, NY: Doubleday, 1979), p. 43.

96 Ibid.

Going Further: Recommended Reading

Rohrick, Lisa M. *Both Feet on God's Path: The Story of Julie Fehr.* Camp Hill, PA: Christian Publications, 1996. Out of print, but available at https://www.lulu.com/en/ca/shop/lisa-m-rohrick/both-feet-on-gods-path/paperback/product-21723476.html.

Smith, Joy Beth. *Party of One: Truth, Longing and the Subtle Art of Singleness.* Nashville, TN: Nelson Books, 2018.

Sneed, Dan. *The Power of a New Identity: Overcoming a Broken Self-Image.* Lancaster, UK: Sovereign World Ltd., 2012.

Tucker, Ruth A. *Extraordinary Women of Christian History: What We Can Learn from Their Struggles and Triumphs.* Grand Rapids, MI: Baker Books, 2016.

The Never-Ending Story:
Passing Faith to the Next Generation

CHAPTER NINE

Viorica's Story

Whatever you heard me teach before an audience of witnesses, I want you to
pass along to trustworthy people who have the ability to teach others too.
—2 Timothy 2:2, VOICE

Oradea, October 2019

The parking lot of Oradea's upscale Hotel Imperio is almost full when I arrive. The evening event won't begin for an hour, but women are already arriving, eager to get a good seat. The rented room in the hotel will hold three hundred, but some suspect many more will try to attend—so they come early. A warm sense of expectation and camaraderie hangs in the air. Women greet each other and hurry to find a seat.

Most of the women here have one thing in common—they have been invited by Viorica. Vio, as many call her, is an unpretentious woman who once a year gathers her disciples to this alumni-style celebration. To be an alumna of one of Viorica's groups is a badge of belonging among women in the churches in Oradea. It would be impossible to estimate how many women are actually represented by the three hundred present for this event, because many of them have groups of their own. New groups are popping up all the time across the Banat region of Romania where Viorica lives.

I find a seat. It occurs to me that the women here tonight, the women in Viorica's study groups, are my fourth generation. My mind moves backwards in time: Viorica was discipled by Ica during the late nineties. Ica was discipled by Nicoleta during the early nineties, who, in turn, was discipled by me in the eighties. Four generations.

reGeneration

Training the Next Generation, 1986–1989

During the eighties, six courageous women from the Pentecostal church in Oradea gathered regularly to study the Bible with teachers from Vienna who came to mentor women.[97] The group gathered, always watchful for secret police in the street. Sometimes, across the street from the apartment block where we met, they'd see a man sitting in an unmarked car or someone wearing dark glasses leaning up against the building as if to make his presence obvious. If a woman in the group saw anything suspicious, she would continue walking, circling back later to see if it was now safe to enter the building where we were meeting.

Nearly every time we met, I would take a folded, metre-square piece of brown butcher paper from my suitcase or tear a page out of my notebook. The women would gather around the paper, which I'd spread on the table. With a black marker, I'd draw a circle in the middle of the paper and write my name, or the names of other travellers from Vienna, in it. From that circle emanated six spokes, and at the end of each spoke was a circle in which I wrote the name of one of the six woman in the room.

The women knew what the diagram was about. It was the Apostle Paul's strategy for multiplying leaders. To his disciple, Timothy, he said, *"Whatever you heard me teach before an audience of witnesses, I want you to pass along to trustworthy people who have the ability to teach others too"* (2 Timothy 2:2, VOICE). We saw three generations in Paul's plan. I was already asking them about the second generation: "Who are the *trustworthy people* (women) to whom you will pass what you learn in this group?"

It was a plan for multiplication, maybe the only way to train the next generation in this hard place. I would press them with the question again: "Tell me, to whom are you passing what you are learning in this group? Who is in the second generation?" It was a rigorous form of accountability with the woman. Nicoleta was in that first group that began in 1985, and Ica was in one of the groups Nicoleta formed near the end of the eighties. Ica invited Viorica to join one of the groups she formed in the early nineties, a third-generation group. This evening I will meet women from Viorica's study groups, the fourth generation.

---

97 Two or three times a year, two women from Vienna would arrive to spend a day or two with the group, sometimes teaching them for six to eight hours a day. Teachers were aware that these eager students had no resources for their own teaching except the Scriptures and whatever notes they took while we taught the group. Looking back, it was very lecture-oriented—not necessarily an educationally sound approach, but the best we could offer given the repressive circumstances.

A hush falls over the room as Vio stands to welcome the women. There is nothing flashy about her. She is a humble woman with little formal education. She speaks softly, her eyes hardly lifting from the podium to engage with her expectant audience. But she speaks with authority.

Ica, Vio's mentor, is in the audience tonight. In 1994, just four years after the Revolution, Ica invited Viorica to join a group of women who were meeting to study a book on marriage.[98] For five years the group met, studying topics like marriage, parenting, discipleship, and how to lead inductive Bible studies. Each time they met, Ica encouraged the participants in her group to start their own groups. She spoke of "investing in the next generation." She encouraged them to teach everything they were learning in the group to another group of *trustworthy* women who, in turn, would teach others also.

The idea filled Viorica with fear. It took nine years, but in 2003 Viorica hesitantly took steps to form a group of women into whose lives she would speak. She struggled to believe she was capable enough to teach anyone. From the beginning, she decided she would never invite anybody to her groups. She asked God to bring the women to her—and they came, from villages around the city of Oradea. Now, sixteen years later, she has led fifty-five groups and invested in 513 women. Each group she forms today meets weekly for four months. Without being told to do so, many of the participants in her groups understand the expectation to form their own group and enter into the generational plan that 2 Timothy 2:2 suggests.

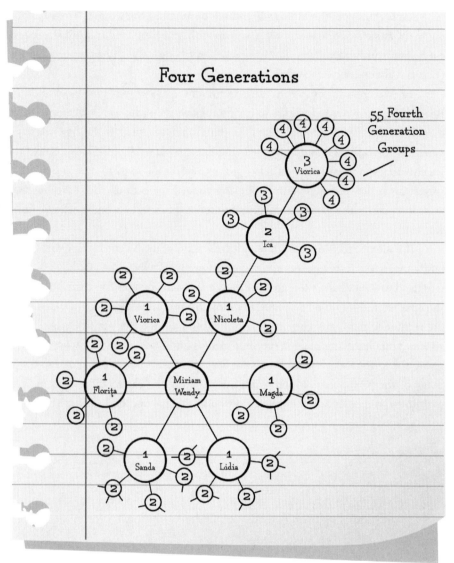

Four Generations

Mission Comes Full Circle

As I stand to speak, it feels like mission has come full circle. Ema, my translator, is not just a skillful linguist. Her presence beside me takes me back thirty-six years (November 1983), to the heavily-shuttered room in the little church on Popa Rusu Street in Bucharest. Six pastors were with me at the table—leaders in the evangelical movement in Romania. Ema's father, Dr. Nick, led the group that day. They were wrestling with the outrageous idea I had just proposed: forming groups like the men's groups that had been meeting, but this time for women!

The idea of training women to serve the church was new to these men. All of them took at face value the Apostle's words, *"Women should remain silent in the churches. They are not allowed to speak.... If they want to inquire about something, they should ask their own husbands at home..."* (1 Corinthians 14:34–35). For these men, the words were timeless instruction: women should learn at home and be quiet.

The men around the table were also wrestling with another complicated reality: it was dangerous for believers to educate the next generation. Gathering a small group was against the law. The men around the table were afraid that if they allowed women's groups to be started, the increased number of participants might expose the program they so deeply treasured. More groups meant more chances of information getting into the wrong hands. What if even one woman inadvertently spoke to a less trustworthy person in the church about the group? What if the training program was uncovered by the authorities?

Tonight I share the words of Dr. Nick, Ema's father, which still echo in my ears: "Miriam, you can't train women! They talk too much!" The double meaning in his statement brought laughter to the men seated around the table thirty-six years ago, and the women in the Imperio Hotel tonight laugh as I retell the story.

Tearing a piece of paper from my notebook, I drew the diagram of 2 Timothy 2:2 which the men already knew so well. I drew a circle with my name in it and six spokes radiating outward. Going around the table, as each man told me his wife's name, I wrote it on the diagram. It was as though he was saying on behalf of his wife, "We're in!"

One year later I began to meet with the wives of six pastors who, at risk and with lots of sacrifice, crossed the country by train to Bucharest to become the first generation of students in the program. Thirty-six years later, I now stand beside Dr. Nick's lovely daughter who translates the story to a room filled with third- and fourth-generation women.

Time to Reflect

1. What missional reality does the picture of Viorica's group members, now numbering more than five hundred, bring to your mind as you think about training leaders for the church in hard places today?

2. What do you already know about this missional reality? Do you know places today where believers dare to gather for training but where education must be done in creative ways? How do they train?

3. Can you think of places in Scripture, especially in the early church of the New Testament, of how training of leaders was carried out in challenging contexts? The next section will further your discussion by looking at a timeless model of education established by Jesus and continued by the Apostle Paul, both of whom were concerned about raising up the next generation of leaders for the church.

Going Deeper

The Great Commission

They waited near the top of one of the highest hills overlooking the Sea of Galilee. They knew it was the right place—they'd been here before. They stared at the lake below, thinking of the miraculous things they had seen Jesus do there. Suddenly, the men saw him walking toward them. As he approached, they fell to their knees and worshipped him. It was the first time some of them had fully acknowledged who he really was, the Son of God. He was with them now in his resurrection body.

His words were direct and full of authority. The disciples felt like there was a crowd of people standing right behind them. It was as though Jesus was speaking to every person who would follow him throughout all of time. His words echoed across the meadow:

> ... go and make disciples of all nations, baptizing them in the name of the Father and of the Son and of the Holy Spirit, and teaching them to obey everything I have commanded you. And surely I am with you always, to the very end of the age.
>
> —Matthew 28:19–20

For All Nations: "Panta ta Ethne"

Jesus told his followers to make disciples of all nations. Matthew, who reported these words of his Commission, used the Greek words, *panta ta ethne*, referring not to political or nation-states as we use the word "nation" today, but to every cultural-linguistic or ethnic (*ethne*) people group on the planet.[99] Today we refer to them as "people groups."[100] Even within a nation-state there are ethnic groups among whom the spreading of the gospel may encounter barriers of understanding (language) and acceptance (culture)—for example, in Spain one will find millions of Spaniards, but hidden among them are nearly a million Arabic-speaking Moroccans and 3.7 million Catalonians who live in the Catalonia region of the country. Language and culture may hide them from the gospel.

Only One Command

Jesus had only one command for them that day—make disciples. That was the mission—plain and simple! What about the other verbs: going, baptizing, and teaching? These three verbs[101] explain what is involved in making disciples. The word "going" (it's assumed we will go) implies we're sent (Romans 10:15). "Baptizing" implies repentance and forgiveness of sins, becoming part of God's family (Acts 2:38–39). "Teaching" makes it clear that Jesus had a lot more in mind than just convincing people to follow him (evangelism). His plan was that his followers would make faithful, maturing disciples who could go on to make others like them.

The word "disciple" comes from the Greek word "to learn." A disciple is a learner. And disciple-making is a fundamentally important educational function of the church. Jesus told his disciples to make learners in every ethnic or cultural/linguistic group on the planet.

While Jesus was on the earth, he showed us what he meant by this command. He modelled what he meant by disciple-making. He preached to big crowds, but he called just a handful out of the crowd and invested his life in them. He could have invested in thousands, but instead he chose twelve. The legacy he left was the transformed lives of a handful of very ordinary people into whom he had invested his life. He then commissioned them to invest their lives in a few more. It was, and is, a very doable plan.

> He preached to big crowds, but he called just a handful out of the crowd and invested his life in them.

---

99 According to UN statistics, there are 195 countries or nation-states in the world today (https://www.thoughtco.com/number-of-countries-in-the-world-1433445). There are many more cultural/linguistic groups—as many as 16,300.

100 To learn more about people groups, go to https://joshuaproject.net/resources/articles/how_many_people_groups_are_there.

101 For those who like grammar, in the Great Commission there is only one imperative verb, "make disciples." There are three participles (-*ing* words telling us how to do it): "going," "baptizing," and "teaching." Christ's command is very clear: make disciples.

An Educational Plan for Hard Places

During the first century, as the church grew, the need for leaders was already a concern. I'm quite certain Jesus discussed with his twelve disciples the importance of developing leaders. I suspect the Apostle Paul must have asked his good friends—who, incidentally, had been discipled by Jesus—what Jesus would have done. Jesus didn't build schools or write books. He invested his life in a few, and they invested in a few more.

People who work in hard places today think about the issue of leaders for the next generation all the time. The church always needs teachers and leaders, but how do you train people to lead in hard places where it's dangerous to gather believers and teach them? That was the dilemma we considered during the eighties in Romania. Paul's advice to Timothy, his young disciple and an emerging leader in the new church, was important for us: *"Whatever you heard me teach before an audience of witnesses, I want you to pass along to trustworthy people who have the ability to teach others too"* (2 Timothy 2:2, VOICE).

These words guided our discussions about how to train leaders in Romania. Many places in the world today face the same challenge, especially where Islamic or atheistic regimes make it almost impossible to build schools and gather people for training. In Romania in the 1980s, we couldn't build schools because the communist regime was fighting the raising up of new leaders. We didn't have many resources—a few titles were translated, printed, and smuggled into the country over the years. We had students who copied an entire textbook by hand because there was only one copy for each group. How do you design education for an emerging church that has few trained leaders, no schools, and few resources? 2 Timothy 2:2 was a good pattern for pastoral training.

The Importance of Accountability

Accountability was a really important part of our relationship with our students. That's why we carried the big square of brown butcher paper in our suitcase. The women would gather around the familiar diagram of 2 Timothy 2:2. The moment of accountability came when we would ask directly, "To whom are you passing everything we teach you? What are the names of women in your own group? You are the first generation. What we teach you, you will teach to the next generation. The second generation will teach the third generation, and the third generation will teach the fourth."

My Children Are Walking in Truth (June 1992)

In 1989, the Berlin Wall* came down and communism crumbled all over Eastern Europe and the Soviet Union. The church emerged from hidden places and stood strong and tall. Freedom brought many changes to how we trained leaders. In early 1992, some of our students began planning the first international conference for women in the history of Romania. It would happen in June. Women in every first-generation group across the country were invited on one condition: they would bring with them the second generation. I had never seen the whites of the eyes of the second generation. It had always been too dangerous for them to meet us, or even to know we came regularly from Vienna.

The day the conference began, we met trains and buses from all over Romania, bringing women to the conference in Oradea. The women, who by now had become like spiritual children, would step off the train, see us waiting, and cry out, "Miriam! Wendy! Lorraine! Come and meet the second generation." And some of the second generation, whom we had never met, would hesitantly say, "I hope it's okay—I have brought a few third-generation women."

Four hundred women—first, second, and a few third-generation disciple-makers—gathered in Oradea. As I stood in front of the crowd of expectant women to open the conference that night, I thought to myself, "If I die tonight, it will have all been worth it." I spoke the words from 3 John 4 over the women: *"I have no greater joy than to hear that my children are walking in truth."*

Another deep-seated joy inside me that night was knowing that in the audience were also women disciple-makers from Bulgaria, Czechoslovakia, Hungary, and the United States. I thought of Christ's Commission to take the message to all nations (*panta ta ethne*), to every linguistic and cultural group on the planet.

To All Peoples

Toronto, 2002

When I answered the phone, I recognized a familiar Romanian voice on the other end. Lidia, a student from the eighties, announced that she was in Toronto for a few days. Sitting in my apartment the next day over dinner, we had lots of catching up to do. Lidia was one of the courageous first-generation women who joined a study group in Timisoara in 1986. She was not a pastor's wife, and now wonders why she was included in the selection of group members for the first-generation group in her city. The other women were wives of pastors—all men who studied in the men's group. But those of us who knew Lidia quickly understood why she was included—she stands out in a crowd as a passionate and gifted woman with obvious leadership gifts.

A New Day, A New Approach (2002)

Over dinner, I learned that for five years Lidia had been leading the ministry among women, passed to her capable hands by visionary, post-Revolution Western leaders. It was time for Romanians to take the reins of leadership. Lidia initiated many changes in the way women's ministry is now done in Romania, changes that make the ministry more culturally sensitive and appropriate for a new day. Teaching does not happen in the top-down, lecture-driven way that the situation in the eighties demanded.

Making disciples is still at the centre of the plan today. But women's ministry in each church is more organic. Women whose gifts are recognized by their local church are responsible for how disciple-making is shaped there. Women are recommended by the local pastor for training in the Priscilla School, an educational model designed by Romanian women to train leaders in the third millennium.

Priscilla School is an intensive thirty-day training for women that is held for five days twice a year over three years. Classes are taught exclusively by Romanian women with ministry experience, each woman teaching in the area of her passion. I hear in Lidia's description of this new model that the pattern of 2 Timothy 2:2 still shapes the training. That brings me much joy!

A New Reality: The Migration of People

My heart is full when Lidia talks about a growing vision among the women for the nations and people groups around them. She speaks of Christ's command to make disciples of "all peoples" (*panta ta ethne*). Lidia is dealing with a new reality in post-communist Romania: the migration of people, something we didn't have to cope with in the eighties. Thousands of Romanians emigrate each year to the West where there are possibilities for a better life. Women in whom she has invested her life are leaving the country.

At first Lidia seems sad as she talks about migration, this thing that is happening everywhere in the majority world. One in five Romanian workers live outside of Romania today. They have left the country because of local poverty and corruption. They are seeking a better life in Western Europe and North America.

At first it was painful for Lidia to accept the emigration of some of the finest women she had trained in the Priscilla School. Sometimes it made her feel sad and even kind of angry. She'd invested so much in these women, only to see them leave Romania in search of a better life somewhere else. But it doesn't take long for women who leave Romania to realize that the society of Western Europe is secular, and the church in the West is weak. God, in His sovereign way, is shuffling the nations, placing Romanians in other European countries—places like Austria, Belgium, France, Germany, Italy, and Spain. Lidia recognizes they have been moved to these places to infect society with a disciple-making movement *for all peoples*.

Women often call for Lidia's help. They ask her to guide them in developing disciple-making ministries for women—not just for other Romanians, but for citizens of the countries where God has placed them. Many of the women they disciple speak only a national language like German or French or Italian. The eyes of Romanian women who have fled from poverty and corruption have been lifted from seeking blessing only for themselves to embracing the lostness of Spaniards, Italians, Belgians, and Germans.

We Are All Children of Abraham

As Lidia tells me her story, she reminds me of God's promises to Abraham. God's words in Genesis 12, which we call the Abrahamic Covenant, are sometimes considered the first statement of the Great Commission.

God promised Abraham, and every generation of God's people after him, a blessed life. He said, *"I will bless you…"* (Genesis 12:2). God's blessing was promised for one reason only—that through Abraham's children and future generations of God's people, *"all peoples on earth will be blessed…"* (Genesis 12:2–3).[102] Israel sometimes forgot why they were blessed, thinking there must be something inherently good in them that made them deserving of God's blessing. They forgot that God had chosen them just because He loved them. God can do that. He chose Israel so that the nations around them would be drawn to God. As they saw God's love lavished on Israel, other nations would seek after God.

God is blessing Romanian Christians today in places around the world where He has placed them, places where the economy is strong and they can flourish. He isn't blessing them because they're special. He's blessing them so that people around them will be drawn to him. God's blessing upon Romanians, and upon all who call

---

102 When Jesus spoke the Great Commission (Matthew 28:19–20) on the Mount of Olives before ascending to heaven, the apostles, well trained in Jewish history, probably intuitively recognized that what he said reached back two thousand years to God's Covenant with Abraham.

themselves children of Abraham,[103] is for one reason only: that all *peoples* on earth will be blessed.

My heart is full as Lidia tells me how God's sovereign movement of people around the world took her to Tajikistan. Tajikistan, a former Soviet republic where Russian is spoken, is now an Islamic republic. In Tajikistan, seventy women longing after God gathered for a week of teaching. Lidia was the biblically equipped teacher for the week. Her words were translated into Russian by a Romanian woman from the Republic of Moldova, also a former Soviet republic, where during communism, Russian and Romanian were the official languages. There could be no mistaking that these two Romanian women had been prepared by God for this moment in time.

The Church in Diaspora

As we talk, Lidia speaks of much more than what is happening in Romania. She keeps using an interesting term, talking about the Romanian church *in diaspora*.* The Greek word *diaspora* is used a few times in the New Testament when the Apostle Luke writes about Christian Jews, a racial and religious minority "scattered" outside of Palestine, usually dispersed by persecution among the nations (Acts 8:4–8, 8:40, 11:19–21).

In the first century, Christians in diaspora spread Christianity all over the Greek and Roman world. Today, Christian Romanian women living outside Romania in diaspora are a racial and religious minority living among the nations. They often ask Lidia for her help in training women in their churches to make disciples right where they live.

That's what has brought Lidia to Canada. Women in the Romanian church in diaspora in Canada invited her to come and teach them how to make disciples in Canada.

Mission Comes Full Circle, 2002

Pieces of the puzzle begin to fall into place as we talk. Lidia is sitting at my table in Toronto, telling me how God is reaching the nations through the Romanian church in diaspora, in places like Canada.

We smile at one another as we realize that nineteen years before, churches in Canada sent me to Romania to plant the seeds of a disciple-making ministry in the receptive hearts of women living in a communist regime. Now in 2002, the

---

103 Galatians 3:29 announces that if you belong to Christ you are a child of Abraham, and therefore an heir of God's two-fold promise: that he will bless you, and that through you, people of all ethnicities (*penta ta ethne*) will be blessed.

Romanian church in diaspora has invited this gifted woman, mentored by disciple-makers from North America during the communist years, to come to Canada and teach Romanian women here how to pass faith to the next generation. Mission has come full circle.

To the Least of These, 2020

My greatest joy, every time I go back to Romania,[104] is spending time with women from the first-generation groups of the eighties. My daughters in faith are getting older, but they are still passionate about Christ's final command to make disciples. They understand that Christ longs to see disciples nurtured among all peoples.

Sanda is another of those beautiful women who was part of the first-generation group in Oradea in the eighties. She grew up in a small village one hour from Oradea—a timid woman without much formal education, but she could read and write. Her husband said she was stubborn enough not to let her lack of education slow her down. She loved to study the Bible, and had leadership gifts others didn't immediately recognize. She quickly grasped the generational concept of 2 Timothy 2:2. In spite of the demands of her growing family and responsibilities as the wife of a leading deacon in the church, she always came to class with her homework done and reports of new groups that she was forming or co-leading with other members of the group.

The accountability factor in the 2 Timothy 2:2 plan was mentioned one day as we bent over the diagram, writing on the square of butcher paper the names of villages where women were leading new groups. As I rocked her fretful new baby in my arms, Sanda whispered to me, "I love my children so much, but I want spiritual children now."

It's 2019. Sanda and I are having tea together. Thirty-four years have passed since the day she mentioned her longing for spiritual children. She wants to update the diagram on the square of brown butcher paper. She talks about the women into whom she has invested her life. Earlier that day, as we toured through the beautiful church where her sons have succeeded her husband, Teo, as pastor, and where she still leads ministries to women, several women grabbed Sanda, pointed to her, and exclaimed, "This is my spiritual mother!" Women in Sanda's church understand the language of generations. She talks with affection about the women in nine second-generation groups she has mentored over the years.

Among those into whose lives she has invested are many whom Jesus would have called *"the least of these"* (Matt 25:40–45). She has groups among women in

---

104 Most recently, a trip in 2018 for eight weeks and a trip in 2019 for five weeks.

prisons, and with orphans—more than one hundred young women who have never been integrated into society. In Romania today, when female orphans turn seventeen, the state withdraws all responsibility for them. Her ministry to these marginalized women reminds me that the Great Commission won't be completed until there are disciples among every people group on earth.

The Roma and the orphans of Romania are two of the people groups the women of Sanda's church are now discipling. Both groups fit the definition of an Unreached People Group. Among the orphans and the Roma, less than two percent are believers, and they, on their own, don't have enough resources to establish a church. They need help from established congregations, women like Sanda and her team, to bring access to Jesus to those who have never heard the Good News.

The Story Never Ends

If following God's call takes you to a hard place where the government doesn't look favourably on training leaders for God's church, don't limit your thinking to all that we associate with formal education—school buildings, libraries, faculties, degree programs, residential campuses, tuition fees, and everything else we associate with school. Don't let the constraints of any regime deter you from investing in future generations.

While he was on the earth, Jesus preached to large crowds. Many responded, but he called a few from the masses and invested in them for three years. It isn't surprising that in the earliest days of the church, Paul reminded young Timothy, *"Whatever you heard me teach before an audience of witnesses, I want you to pass along to trustworthy people who have the ability to teach others too"* (2 Timothy 2:2, VOICE).

Paul invested in people like Timothy, Barnabas, John Mark, Priscilla, and Aquila, always with the understanding that first generation learners would teach the second generation, the second generation would teach the third generation, and the third generation would teach the fourth. A good learner always has her eyes open for reliable people to whom she can pass what she is learning. She understands that leadership formation never ends with her own learning. There is a never-ending reGeneration of faith as reliable people like her pass living faith to the next generation. In turn, the next generation enters the regenerative process, passing all they learn to the next generation. And so it is that resilient faith thrives in hard places.

The Story Comes
Full Circle

CHAPTER TEN

Finding Lucia, October 2018

The narrow asphalt road climbs higher and higher as we drive further into the Apuseni Mountains, part of the western Carpathian Mountains in Romania's Transylvania. The mountainside is brilliant with trees wearing the red, gold, and burnt orange of autumn. As the road snakes through the valley, we occasionally see in the distance a mountain peak already dusted with the first winter snow. We climb higher, passing through picturesque, slow-paced villages where it seems that time stands still. A stork nests on the chimney of a thatched roof cottage. An old woman sits outside her gate in a spot of sunshine, coaxing coarse wool onto spindles. Meadows are mowed by hand with giant scythes. We pass horse-drawn carts piled high with hay being taken to barns outside the village.

Excitement is building inside me as Mircea, my friend and driver, describes our destination, Cabana Lui Puiu (Puiu's Cottages), a retreat centre near the village of Somesul Rece. At the end of this road I will meet Lucia, whose prophetic words thirty-five years ago launched me on this journey. I haven't seen her since the first time I met with an underground group of believers in her home in Cluj, December 1983 (see Chapter 1).

As Mircea drives, my thoughts wander far from what he is saying. I'm remembering my first visit to Romania in 1983, sitting in the dimly lit living room of a courageous pastor who hosted not only fellow pastors from the towns and villages surrounding Cluj, but a foreign teacher from Vienna and a woman from Canada, both of whom had declared at the border that they were tourists. If our secret gathering that night had been discovered, he might have gone to prison for hosting us. Our gathering was criminal—a meeting the authorities feared would breed revolution. The presence of foreigners would make the punishment even more severe.

That night, the pastor's daughter, Lucia, had seen beyond my own naiveté and innocently stated the obvious: "Miriam, men in Romania cannot imagine a woman teaching them anything, especially from the Scriptures. Why don't you do some-thing with women in Romania?"

Now, thirty-five years later, I want to find Lucia.

Mircea must have thought I was crazy when I asked if he might know the pastor in whose apartment I had met other pastors in 1983. Thirty-five years had passed—it was a long shot, but I was trying to connect the dots. I wanted to find Lucia.

Thirty-five years ago, young Mircea wasn't yet a pastor, not yet part of the train-ing program. He worked as an engineer in a factory and served as a lay minister in his church. I first met him, a young and enthusiastic pastor, in 1985, two years after meeting Lucia.

As I prepared to write this book, I reread many letters written to my mother during the eighties. One letter, written in 1986,[105] three years after my first trip to Romania, described teaching women in the town of Ocna Mures. The group includ-ed Mircea's young wife. Several of Mircea's friends, when delivering their wives to the meeting in Ocna Mures, had told Mircea they recognized me from a meeting three years before. I recorded the observation in the letter to my mother and never thought about it again.

Thirty-two years later, as I read through the letters I'd written my mother, I realized the pastors who crossed paths in Ocna Mures must have met me in Cluj in December 1983. Perhaps the pastors in Lucia's home that night were now in Mir-cea's circle of friends, and perhaps one of them would know where Lucia was today. I sent an email to Mircea.

Mircea enthusiastically explored my clues: a woman named Lucia who was in her early twenties in 1983 (now probably approaching sixty). She spoke French, worked at the train station in Cluj, and still lived at home with her parents and sib-lings at that time. Several days later Mircea announced excitedly in an email, "I have found Lucia! I will take you to see her when you come to Romania in September."

Now, Mircea eases his car into a parking stall in front of a wood-framed house that matches the cabins known as Puiu's Cottages, scattered across the mountain property. We sit for a moment in the mid-day sun and admire the brilliant fall co-lours on the mountainside across the valley. It's a breathtaking backdrop for Cabana Lui Puiu, the retreat centre where Mircea says we will find Lucia.

Suddenly there's a tap on the window. I look up through the glass into the face of a beautiful woman, now thirty-five years older than the young woman in my

---

105 The letter was one of many letters found in my mother's home after her death. I had written lengthy letters during the eighties to people in my "Inner Circle," a group of praying family and friends in Canada. The letters became a reliable source of data for writing this book.

memory. I've carried that face in my memory for decades. This is the woman who, guided by the Spirit of God, spoke a simple word into the ear of a woman ten years older than her—a word that would change the course of my life. She planted the seed of something far greater than me and shaped the destiny of many.

I step out of the car into her warm embrace. It is a holy moment. Those around us watch silently, acknowledging the wonder of the journey, honouring the moment as Lucia and I embrace.

Epilogue
WHEN BEECH TREES BEAR PEARS

The Walls Come Down—November 1989

The Trabi Trail

From my place in the driver's seat, as far as my eye could see, there was a line of East German-made Trabants heading west on the M1 motorway toward Hungary's border with Austria. It was a very strange sight for me as we headed east toward Budapest, away from the border we had just crossed.

I had an eye for Trabants. They made me laugh. I thought they were ugly. And now I saw them, kilometre after kilometre of them, moving slowly down the highway toward us, smoke belching from the exhaust. The Trabant was a product of the communist era, its body made of pressed garbage, a two-stroke engine like a lawnmower, fuelled with a mixture of gasoline and oil. It had no fuel gauge or seatbelts, and couldn't exceed 50 kilometres an hour, not even going down a hill. And yet there was a certain fraternity among Eastern European owners of Trabants, something I had learned from Romanian drivers who, when they passed another Trabant, would often slow down, turn quickly around, and go back to meet the owner of one of these beloved, garbagy cars. They knew the driver would inevitably be waiting for them, having quickly pulled over for a friendly exchange.

Usually the license plates on the M1 all indicated Hungarian or Austrian origins. But today we passed Trabant after Trabant, all with East German plates, chugging along in an endless line, heading west toward Hungary's border with Austria. We noticed and commented on it, thinking nothing more about it as we continued toward Budapest, where we found a safe place to park our car and caught a train, heading further east into Romania.

Our train pulled into Oradea around 6:00 p.m., giving us enough time to walk to the pastor's home and wait till darkness fell. Only then would it be safe for someone to take us to the place where the women would meet that night.

November 9, 1989

Night had fallen. As we crawled without speaking into the back seat of the car, I recognized the driver, the husband of one of our students. He sat at the wheel, waiting anxiously without lights, hoping the secret police hadn't seen us dash from the back door of the house, across the back alley, and into his car. He didn't turn on his driving lights until we were settled in the back and he had driven from the alley onto the main street.

The minute we merged onto the busier road, the driver turned and whispered into the back seat, "I just heard on Radio Free Europe that the Berlin Wall is coming down!" He gripped the wheel as the shock of his words filled the car. He continued, "Something's also happening in Bulgaria. President Zhivkov has resigned."

I leaned forward, hoping my face wasn't visible to anyone in the street, and whispered, "Brother, does this news give you hope for Romania?"

Slowly and with pain on his face, he leaned into the steering wheel and groaned quietly, "Oh sister, we have no hope in this country!"

In a sense, he was right. There was little about which a Romanian could be hopeful on this night, though in Berlin people from both East and West were dancing on the Berlin Wall at the opening of Checkpoint Charlie.[106] Border officials were allowing Germans to go back and forth. Dancers on the wall seemed drunk with euphoria as they celebrated the cracks appearing in the Wall.

During the next two weeks in Romania, we heard nothing more. The Ceausescu government had doubled its efforts to jam radio signals and block any news coming from Western Europe into Romania.[107] The only thing Romanians were talking about was that food rations for the upcoming winter would be even less adequate than they'd been last year. During the summer, several of my colleagues from Vienna had been arrested, interrogated, and given twenty-four hours' notice to leave the

---

106 On the night of November 9, 1989, three thousand West Berliners came to Checkpoint Charlie and several hundred East Berliners came to the east side's Checkpoint Friedrichstraße. While the people in the West cried "Let us in," those in the East cried "Let us out." At 11:00 p.m., Checkpoint Friedrichstraße was closed by the East German border command. But before midnight, the border was completely open and East Germans were allowed to enter the West. After more than twenty-eight years, the Berlin Wall was open and people from East Germany could leave if they wanted to do so.

107 Though we often visited the American Embassy while in Bucharest, hoping to get news about what was happening in the West, we found that news was censored even there. Copies of the *International Herald Tribune* were always two or three weeks old. In Romania, we felt cut off from news, having no way of knowing what was happening in the rest of the world.

country with the accusation that "Romanian young people don't need your perverted philosophies."

Meanwhile, peaceful revolution was happening in almost all of the countries of the Eastern Bloc, as Gorbachev's plans for *glasnost*[108] and *perestroika*[109] were being tested. On November 18, ten days after the opening of the Berlin Wall, Ceausescu closed the border between Hungary and Romania. No travellers were allowed to enter or leave Romania. He had no intention of following the lead of the countries surrounding Romania that were giving a nod to capitalism.

My Cover Is Blown

I left Romania on November 17. A rigorous interrogation at the Hungarian border made me realize that security was getting tight in Romania. It seemed that my cover as a tourist, carrying the business card of a travel agent, might no longer work, although I had successfully used this approach to get in and out of Romania for six years.

As a border guard searched our luggage, he found my teaching notebook tucked in among damp towels and dirty laundry. The guard became noticeably belligerent. He paged through my teaching notebook, obviously wishing he knew English. I was worried, because sprinkled through my teaching notes were coded messages: names of medicines believers had asked us to bring on our next visit, delivery instructions for book smugglers who would soon bring more teaching materials into the country, and names and addresses of families in great need, living close to starvation. I would decode the information as soon as I got back to Vienna.

He laid my notebook on the seat beside me and continued to search my suitcase, squinting into a small container of shampoo as though I might have hidden something there, opening every zipper on my cosmetic case, and finally lifting the false bottom of the suitcase. By then, everything in my suitcase had been dumped on the floor. Another guard had already taken our passports into the train station. Frustration was written all over the face of the customs official. He left with my notebook and was gone for thirty minutes.

---

108 *Glasnost*, initiated by Mikhail Gorbachev in the Soviet Union during the 1980s, was a policy of more open, consultative government and wider dissemination of information, certainly a new posture for Eastern Bloc countries.

109 *Perestroika*, the idea of restructuring the economic and political system in the Soviet Union and its satellite states, was actively promoted by Mikhail Gorbachev. It originally referred to increased automation and labor efficiency, but was particularly distasteful to Ceausescu because it pointed to the end of central planning. Ceausescu's plan for "systematization,"* a centrally planned scheme to reduce the number of Romania's villages by half by the year 2000, had led to the destruction of thousands of villages. Work camps and agricultural communes replaced the villages.

When he returned, an English-speaking guard was with him. I recognized the guard from previous border crossings. He laid my notebook on the seat beside me as he looked me in the eye and said with a loud and menacing voice, "We know who you are! You're a Canadian who speaks French. You were born in China. You live in Vienna now. You call yourself a travel agent when we ask your profession." Looking down his long nose at me, he scoffed, "You travel here many times a year. That's ridiculous! Who would visit Romania more than once?!" He rose to his feet to leave as he shoved the notebook into my hands. With a sarcastic edge in his voice he shouted, "Next time you come to Romania—and I'm sure it will be soon—bring me some spy novels in English!"

He left the compartment, and through the dirty windows we saw him step off the train. One minute later, the train lurched forward, heading to the Hungarian side of the border. I was shaken from the search and by the insinuation in his final statement. Were my days in communist Romania over? They seemed to have my number.

Communism Is Crumbling

Only as we neared Vienna did I remember the "Trabi invasion" we had seen ten days earlier on the M1 motorway on our way to Budapest. By the thousands, East Germans had already begun to travel across Czechoslovakia[110] to border-crossing points with Hungary.

They had heard that Hungarian officials would let them cross at the Hagyeshalom border crossing between Hungary and Austria. Rumour had it that once they'd crossed the Hungarian side of the border and the two kilometres of no man's land, the Nickelsdorf border patrol on the Austrian side would turn a blind eye to East German drivers in their Trabants. These people were taking no chances that the opportunity to get out of East Germany would last forever.

The Fourteenth Romanian Communist Party Congress

Back in Vienna, our hearts were still in Romania. We were glued to TV and radio for any news that might leak out now that Ceausescu had closed all borders with the West. Within two days of our return, November 20th, the Fourteenth Romanian Communist Party Congress began in Bucharest. Every delegate to the Congress knew that the Berlin Wall had been breached two weeks earlier. News that the old regime was collapsing in East Germany, Czechoslovakia, and Bulgaria was in the minds of the 3300 carefully chosen delegates who had gathered to re-elect Nicolae

---

110 After the Revolution of 1989, Czechoslovakia was divided into two countries, the Czech Republic and the Republic of Slovakia.

Ceausescu—the only candidate on the ballot for president. Stories of Czechs in Prague chanting "Ceausescu will be next!" had seeped into the Congress.

Sixty-seven standing ovations punctuated Ceausescu's five-hour opening remarks that day, though most of the ovations were written into the script of his speech and executed on cue. The delegates applauded as he exaggerated the triumph of scientific socialism in Romania. He reminded them of the undeniable necessity of the dictatorship of the Party and the glorious way their *Conducator* (Great Leader) had erased poverty in the country. Apparently, he'd wept when he heard that the Berlin Wall was crumbling. In his lengthy speech, he made it very clear that Romania would not follow the lead of surrounding communist countries in their return to capitalism.

When Beech Trees Bear Pears

Ceausescu stood at the podium before his audience, as they chanted his name and roared their approval. "Chow-uh-shes-koo! Chow-uh-shes-koo!"[111] His voice was tired and raspy as he railed on and on in praise of himself. The delegates rose to their feet and chanted in unison, "Down with capitalism!" The speech continued for hours, as he harangued against capitalism and raised high the accomplishments of communism during his twenty-six-years as president. It was like an interminable pep rally.

In one final attempt to convince the delegates, with his clenched fist raised toward heaven he shrieked into the microphone a final statement of communist propaganda, vowing that the Soviet-style reform happening in countries around them would come to Romania only when "beech trees bear pears."[112]

In the days that followed, as revolution began to boil, theatre students in Bucharest hung every pear they could find in the city on the barren trees that lined the

---

111 The "personality cult" of Ceausescu was patterned after what he had seen in the regimes of China's Mao Zedong and North Korea's Kim Il Sung. When Ceausescu met the North Korean leader in Pyongyang in October 1988, he watched as half a million North Koreans prostrated themselves before their Great Leader and his guest. It became a model that Ceausescu implemented in staged rallies. Four thousand party members would rise to their feet and loudly chant the leader's name in unison as though they worshipped him. The "personality cult," staged by Ceausescu himself, camouflaged the underlying hatred of Romanians for their ruthless dictator. Ceausescu had nearly erased the national debt, but he'd done so at the expense of the Romanian people, whom he kept near starvation for much of the 1980s. Staged rallies suggested to the West that he was a beloved and popular president, a lie much of the world believed.

112 Robert C. Toth, "Romania, Death of a Dictator: Barren Trees Sported Pears and Ceausescu Fell," *Los Angeles Times*, December 27, 1989. This final shout by Ceausescu and the response of theatre students was reported by Vladimir Tismaneanu, at the time a resident scholar at the Foreign Policy Research Institute in Philadelphia. He had learned about it in a phone call from Romania on Christmas night, 1989. The original words in Ceausescu's speech have been quoted in varying translations.

capital's main streets. Historians suggest that this final shout by the dictator was what precipitated his fall. This mockery by the students so infuriated Ceausescu that he ordered the Securitate, his secret police, to find the perpetrators and kill them. Reportedly, more than a hundred died. But the courage of students was inflamed by this turn of events. It was students who courageously began the catcalls that interrupted Ceausescu's final speech from the balcony on Palace Square less than one month later on December 22. On Christmas Day, Ceausescu and his wife Elena were executed.

According to the official version, the Ceausescus were shot by firing squad in an undisciplined volley, many soldiers shooting before the official order was given. Whether it is fact or not, rumour has it that their embalmed bodies were taken back to Bucharest and buried among the graves of those who died while fighting to overthrow them. Mark Almond, a British historian of Romania, believes that their graves were covered with concrete to make "discovery rather than resurrection more difficult."[113]

The tyrants were executed, but they were never called to account for their crimes. They were never tried for their deliberate impoverishment of a rich country and an industrious people, the sacrifice of an entire generation's well-being, the suppression of all dissent, unimaginable brutality toward any who opposed them, and the humiliation of an entire people, especially of Christians, year after year, for many decades.[114]

God Is With Us
No story of Romania's 1989 Christmas Revolution would be complete without acknowledging the bravery of believers in that dark hour. On the first Sunday of November 1989, believers across Romania spent the day in prayer and fasting for their country. Rumours of upheaval across Eastern Europe had leaked into Romania via radio, but the situation in their own country was so bad, they dared not dream that such changes would come to them.

The Power of Prayer
For ten years before the revolution, women in groups of six or eight met to pray that God would bring freedom to meet openly. Because the women met in secret, they didn't know that others were likewise laying their longing for freedom before the Lord. After the revolution, they discovered similar prayer groups had existed all over Romania. Young revolutionaries among the student population in Timisoara took

113 Mark Almond, *The Rise and Fall of Nicolae and Elena Ceauşescu* (London: Chapmans Publishers Ltd., 1992), p. 236.
114 Ibid., p. 231–232.

up arms with prayer, not weapons, crying out to God to turn his face to Romania—to bring revival, and bring it through Timisoara.[115]

God heard their prayers. Timisoara, a city on Romania's western border with Serbia, became the reference point of God's intervention in Romania. I've often stood on Timisoara's main square between the Orthodox cathedral and the Opera House and remembered the story of a Hungarian Reformed Church pastor named Laszlo Tokes. Today if you visit his church, not far from the main square, you will find on its grey stone walls a plaque in four languages that says, "Here began the revolution that felled a dictator."

The Power of God's Presence in His People

Some pastors compromised with the state during the communist years. One who did not was Laszlo Tokes, to whom God gave understanding of what could happen if the church correctly perceived its identity in the world. Tokes became a threat to the regime as people, especially young people, came to faith and were discipled. His church grew from insignificance to five thousand strong, a force that even the Securitate could not withstand.

The secret police realized that killing Tokes would only make him a martyr. They decided to remove him from his parish in Timisoara to a remote village outside the city where he would have no influence. They set the date of eviction for December 15. On Sunday, December 10, during morning worship, Tokes urged his people to be present on eviction day. He asked them to "Come, be peaceful, but be witnesses."[116]

They came. They stayed. They shouted their secret dreams: "Liberty! Freedom!" They sang a patriotic song banned by the regime for years, "Awake, Romania!" Christians from all over the city rallied and prayed that what was happening there in Timisoara would be the beginning of the end of the tyranny of Ceausescu's regime.

In a bloody arrest on December 17, Tokes and his wife, Edith, were taken away. The crowd moved to the central square of Timisoara where the Communists finally responded with brute force, opening fire on the protesters. The truth may never be known about how many were killed—probably hundreds.

---

115 Interview by Ellen Vaughn on September 18, 1990, with one of my former doctoral students, Gelu Paul, as reported in *Being the Body* by Charles Colson and Ellen Vaugh (Nashville, TN: Thomas Nelson, 2003), p. 246.

116 Laszlo Tokes tells his own story of the events leading to his arrest in Timisoara on December 15 in *The Fall of Tyrants: The Incredible Story of One Pastor's Witness, the People of Romania, and the Overthrow of Ceausescu* (Wheaton, IL: Crossway Books,1990). Chuck Colson and Ellen Vaughn bring order to the confusing details of those days of revolution in Timisoara in their book *Being the Body* (Nashville, TN: Thomas Nelson, 2003).

It's very certain that God was present on the town square of Timisoara between the Orthodox church and the Opera House. He was present in the prayers of God's people and in the people of God who decided to stand for truth, even if it meant the loss of their lives.

As tragic as Romanian history has been, the communist era raised suffering to an unprecedented level. But the disappearance from the scene of Nicolae and Elena Ceausescu in 1989 seemed to solve very little in Romania. As I walked the streets of Bucharest and Timisoara in October 2019, I wondered if, although the Ceausescus had now been dead for thirty years, their mentality and ambitions lived on in others.

I Had to Go Back—Bucharest 2019

The late afternoon sun spreads its soft rays over Piața Revoluției (Revolution Square), a vast square in Bucharest where the former Royal Palace and home of the Central Committee of the Romanian Communist Party are found. It is a sober moment for me, and I stand and reflect. Nearly thirty years ago, tanks rolled, streets ran with blood, and the uprising against Ceausescu happened on this square, known then as Piața Palatului (Palace Square). Historians call what happened in Bucharest in December 1989 the singular event that terminated the Cold War* in Europe.[117]

Here on December 21, 1989, from the balcony of the Royal Palace overlooking Palace Square, Ceausescu gave his last speech to an orchestrated rally of impoverished miners and factory workers who had been bribed and bullied to attend the rally, responding on cue with deafening roars of "Chow-uh-shes-koo! Chow-uh-shes-koo!" Here the crowd turned on him. Students at the back of the crowd were emboldened when news that the revolution in Timisoara, though bloody, had turned a corner against Ceausescu. They began to boo. Catcalls from the back of the crowd punctuated the air and were briefly heard by the television audience before technicians realized what was happening and switched to their well-used soundtrack of canned applause.

The rally was intended to present to official media that Ceausescu had strong support from the people. Instead it erupted into the popular revolt that led to the end of the regime—and the lives of the Ceausescus.

---

117 Robert Kaplan, *In Europe's Shadow: Two Cold Wars and a Thirty-Year Journey Through Romania and Beyond* (New York: Random House, 2016), p. 46.

I Had to Go Back

For some reason, I need to go back to Palace Square, now Revolution Square. I set out to find it on a warm afternoon in October 2019. Poring over the city map, I search in vain for Revolution Square. I know it is close to hotels where I used to stay. As soon as I see the legendary Intercontinental Hotel on Piaţa Universităţii (University Square), I realize I am in familiar territory, but I'm not sure which direction to walk. I buy a soft, delicious brioche at a hole-in-the wall bakery kiosk and eat it standing in the shadow of the hotel.

A young woman sitting on a metre-high marble wall in front of the hotel hardly looks up from her cell phone when I stop to ask if she can point the way to Revolution Square. When she finally looks up, she has a blank look on her face as she says, "I have *no* idea where to find… what was that? Revolution Square?" Her face suggests she also has no idea what revolution such a square might commemorate. She googles Piaţa Revoluţiei and shows me a satellite image on her phone. I am close. She returns to more important things on her cell phone as though she has just pointed the way to the nearest McDonalds.

Five minutes later I stand on Revolution Square, looking at what was supposed to be the centrepiece of the square, Memorial al Renaşterii, the Memorial of Rebirth that honours the victims of the Romanian Revolution of 1989. I feel a sense of hopelessness as I look at the monument that has been erected there to commemorate the 1989 losses—around one thousand lives. The monument features a twenty-five-metre-high pillar reaching to the sky, upon which is impaled a metal "crown."[118] Its name, Memorial of Rebirth, alludes to the hoped-for rebirth of Romania as a nation after the collapse of Ceausescu's dictatorship.

The monument is in great disrepair. Two young boys are using its concrete base as a skateboard launch pad, which explains why much of the thin marble at the bottom of the pillar is now missing. It has been broken by the repeated impact of skateboards over the years and never repaired, exposing the ugly innards of the marble pillar.

---

118 Described by some as a "potato skewered on a stake" or an "olive on a toothpick," the controversial monument is now guarded around the clock because it is so often defaced with graffiti. In 2012, the bottom of the metal "crown" was defaced with a splash of bright red paint, so inaccessibly high on the pillar it has never been removed.

Revolution Square is a mishmash of cheap reproductions of formerly magnificent works of art destroyed during the communist years,[119] cluttered with memorials and statues, some of them overgrown by weeds and vines, and surrounded by relentless traffic, with horns shrieking as vehicles circle past on Calea Victoriei. The disrepair of the square and the misuse of the monument as a skateboard launchpad are a depressing metaphor for a population struggling to recover its noble past and self-respect but never quite succeeding.

I stand there, remembering this city as it was in the eighties. For thirty years since the revolution, my mind has replayed images of long lines for bread and fuel, painted in shades of black and grey. In my mind, I see people standing in the early morning cold, waiting in front of shops with empty shelves, drawn there by the rumour of a possible delivery of meat or eggs or cheese. People waited in shifts, sometimes all night, only to go home emptyhanded.

When I first came to Bucharest in 1983, buses didn't run on diesel but on the much cheaper and more dangerous methane gas, with tanks attached to the roofs. The city was often dark because of power cuts. People were starving to death and freezing in their apartments.

I returned to Bucharest a few weeks after the Revolution at Christmas in 1989 to visit Palace Square and honour the revolutionaries who died fighting Ceausescu. But I felt like I'd never taken time to really come to terms with my experiences. The more years that passed, the more I needed to return to Bucharest and validate the memories. They were an important part of the stories I wanted to tell. I had to go back.

A Validation of Memories

I've scheduled four days in Bucharest, just to walk the streets and visit the sites that figure prominently in my memories. My memories from the eighties are the reference point as I wander the streets now, thirty years later.

I keep telling myself that it's unfair to suggest that nothing has changed in Romania since 1989. A lot has—certainly the atmosphere in the city. Before the Revolution, a sense of fear and suspicion hung everywhere. One half of the country was informing on the other half. If people spoke the name of their dictator, they whispered it, afraid that mention of his name might be picked up by a listening device in the street. Registration of privately-owned typewriters was required, along with

---

119 For example, the bronze statue of King Carol I on his horse was destroyed by the communist government in 1948 because of its association with the monarchy. The reproduction standing in its place isn't nearly as lovely, but it represents an attempt by artists to replace what was lost during the communist era.

the owner's fingerprints. To a large extent, the sense of despair and futility that per-meated the lives of people in the streets is now gone. But in essence, it feels to me as though everyday life happens much as it did before the revolution

Walking from downtown to my hotel near the North Train Station, a sadness comes over me as I navigate the broken sidewalks, chipped concrete, garbage, and abandoned buildings. I feel a general sense of abandonment, realizing that even after thirty years, the city is still broken by its communist past. Parks, once reasonably cared-for places where citizens found respite from the harshness of life in a commu-nist regime, are now in derelict state: tall weeds, graffiti on stone benches that are missing planks, virtually empty.

Along the way there are flower shops, bookstores, and cafes with elegant names like The Temple, Frufru, or La Muse, trying desperately to suggest a civilized connection with Europe. The city of silence of thirty years ago is now a city of car and bus drivers permanently laying on their horns. Every pedestrian is busy on a smartphone. The faces of the young seem empty. The city feels anxious to me.

As I push past the Roma* women in the area outside my hotel and take the lit-tle cage-like lift to my room on the fourth floor, it seems that, even thirty years later, the transition from Ceausescu's communism to something else isn't over. Bucharest is still a broken city.

Earlier in the day, I sat for several hours in Starbucks on Calea Victoriel with Diana, a beautiful woman just old enough to remember Romania under Ceausescu, but young enough to have walked with several generations since the Revolution. She loves the youth of this city of unspeakable brokenness. She describes Bucharest as a troubled city that never sleeps, but lives in perpetual darkness. The older gener-ations seem inflicted with emotional amnesia, refusing to remember where they've come from. No one wants to talk about their communist past. Younger generations have no idea where they come from, working till six each evening and then going to bars to numb themselves against the pointlessness of life. She wonders aloud how the Good News informs such times.

A City in Rebirth

I try to find the mournful hotels where we stayed in the eighties for thirty-five dol-lars a night. We always felt the presence of the Securitate, who monitored every word foreign guests spoke in the hotels, restaurants, or even on the street. Many of the old hotels we stayed in have either been demolished or claimed by chains like Hilton and Ramada, rebuilt as sterile but glitzy places for the chic to gather.

I find the Union Hotel, not far from Piața Revoluției. In the eighties it was a sleazy three-star hotel that foreigners like I could afford. More importantly, it was within walking distance of the small church on Popa Rusu Street where we met the women in Bucharest.

I stand on the sidewalk outside the hotel. My eyes rise to the sixth floor, where we were always given the same room. We assumed this was because the sixth-floor rooms were outfitted with hidden microphones so the secret police could eavesdrop on foreign customers. At night we often addressed sarcastic comments to the upper corner of the room, complaining to "Boris" when we didn't have heat or hot water, chastising him for the hotel's shoddy standards. Was it more than coincidence that the lacking amenity (hot water or heat) would often be turned on within minutes? Someone was listening.

The Securitate were identified not by uniforms but by their constant presence in the lobby, never standing far from Reception, listening to every question guests addressed to the woman behind the desk. Usually we were on our way to the little church on Popa Rusu Street, not far from the hotel. Hoping to confuse the man standing beside us at the desk (whom we suspected was planted there to discover our plans for the evening), we would ask if the National Theatre was within walking distance, hoping he wouldn't follow us as we walked from the Union Hotel to the little church.

There, six women would be waiting eagerly for us and an evening of learning together. We always walked to the church by a circuitous route, never going directly there, always checking over our shoulders to be sure the man hovering near the reception desk wasn't following us. Arriving at the grey metal gate of the church, we always made one more loop around the block to be sure we weren't being followed.

The Church in Strada Popa Rusu
Now I want to find the little church where our secret—well, perhaps not-so-secret—Bucharest group was birthed in 1983. On this bright Sunday in October 2019, I convince a taxi driver to help me find 22 Popa Rusu Street. He is quite sure there is no church at that location. Apart from the cross rising on the side of the building behind the fence, it still isn't obvious there is a church behind the grey gate.

In the eighties, there had been no cross. During the eighties, the only cars in the street outside the church had been the unmarked vehicles of secret police, who intended their cars to be a menacing deterrent for anyone who thought about walking through the gate. We always hoped our old clothes, bent shoulders, and plodding steps signalled to the secret police the arrival of several old but faithful woman at the church.

Today, the cars of Sunday morning parishioners line the narrow street in front of the small church.[120] Residents in the area certainly know there's a church in the neighbourhood.

I pause outside the gate to take a picture and then go through it into the courtyard. In the eighties, I was only in the sanctuary of the church once, sitting in the balcony so no one would see me. My purpose in being here today is to find the little room where, thirty-five years ago, six pastors agreed that their wives could become the first group of women students.

After the service, I ask the pastor and several of the old people having coffee in the courtyard if the room still exists, but I realize that the meetings held in the eighties were such a well-kept secret that no one alive now knows what I am talking about. I ask where I might find a dark little room where the underground pastoral training classes would have met during communism. No one knows about the meetings. The pastor reminds me that he was three years old in 1983, and nine years old at the time of the Revolution. He tells me to wander freely through the church and see what I can find.

It doesn't take long to find the room. I know it as soon as I see it—to the left off the courtyard, now a brightly painted Sunday school room. Memories flood back as I stand in the room. I see the small closet at the back where meals were prepared for us when we met to study, six women sitting around the table, the shades drawn tightly on the windows. Because of our proximity to the street, we spoke with whispered voices.

"You Can Like It, Hate It, or Use It"

Bucharest's Palace of Parliament is another place I need to return to during my days in Bucharest in 2019. Construction on the Palace of the People (renamed the Palace of the Republic before receiving its current name after the Revolution)[121] was begun

---

120 During communist times, the authorities tried to make it difficult for Christians to attend church. Supposedly to save on gasoline, a rule existed that each weekend, especially Sundays, only half of the cars could be driven. Drivers with even-numbered license plates could drive their cars one Sunday, and on the next Sunday, drivers with odd-numbered plates could drive. These restrictions and the unpredictability of public transportation made even getting to church a challenge, part of the regime's intentional plan to intimidate Christians.

121 The name change happened when Ceausescu, who was excessively paranoid, suddenly realized that if it was called the Palace of the People, some Romanians might one day think that they had the right to make use of the palace. In fact, very little of the area was intended for citizens' use—only the square in front of the massive building where Ceausescu pictured 250,000 could assemble to praise the *Conducator* and his wife as they stood on the balcony of their palace.

during the eighties, conceived by the maniacal dictator and his wife, Nicolae and Elena Ceausescu, as a monument to their glory. They intended it to be their place of residence for the rest of their lives, but were executed before they could move in.

As a free-standing complex, only the Pentagon is bigger than the Palace of Parliament. It is seven times the size of Louis XIV's Versailles palace. Buckingham Palace could fit inside the areas set aside for underground car parking at the back.[122] Rising eighty-four metres above ground, its fifteen floors don't seem as high as they really are. The five storeys below ground contain lead-lined bunkers that were to house the Ceausescu family if a nuclear war happened. Tunnels with an electric light railway that could remove important people from danger are part of the underground design.[123] Ceausescu prided himself that everything in the palace was made exclusively with products from Romania: panelling from ancient Romanian oak, chestnut, and cherry trees, marble from the Apuseni Mountains, and crystal from Romanian mines.

Before we go through security, the guide reminds us that no one should wander from the tour she is leading. With these directly stated words, she leads us through security into Ceausescu's grandiose palace, now the Palace of Parliament, the seat of Romania's government. A very small part of it is used for parliamentary halls, offices, and a conference centre. Much of it sits empty and in disrepair—leaking roofs, water damage, and frayed carpets.

The opening lines of the guided tour are, "You can like it, hate it, or use it!" Her words are an attempt to ward off the angry sentiments of tourists who know that this monstrosity at the heart of Bucharest isn't a place of pride for Romanians. They know that Ceausescu removed everything in its way during construction— people, historic buildings, and homes. Its location in the heart of the city meant that large portions of the historic centre of Bucharest were bulldozed to make way for standardized apartment blocks meant for the President's *apparatchiks*,* government buildings including an outlandish Civic Centre, and the palace itself. Some say that one fifth of Bucharest's downtown area was bulldozed. More than forty thousand people were removed by force from their homes—often given only six hours' notice, and sometimes less, before their homes were destroyed. Historic buildings, monasteries, and beautiful churches were either demolished or moved to other sites.

Our guide walks a thin line during the tour, trying to avoid details that might inflame the minds of tourists like me who know that the construction of the palace in the eighties happened on the backs of hapless citizens, while pointing out the

---

122 Almond, *Rise and Fall*, p. 153.
123 Ibid., p. 170.

lavishness of the marble hallways, hand-cut crystal chandeliers in every room,[124] and the oak-panelled room where Ceausescu and his politburo were intended to meet around an oak table large enough for all sixty council members to sit. When our guide points out Ceausescu's chair in this meeting room, she casually mentions the escape door hidden under panelling behind his chair, connected to the bunkers by a lift, just in case he needed to escape. His paranoia is built into many aspects of the palace, though not obvious to the unsuspecting tourist. This part of her tour begins to bring back memories I've long forgotten.

As the ninety-minute guided tour comes to an end, our guide explains that on this tour we've seen only four percent of the building. Our tour won't include the five underground floors of the 265,000 square foot complex, places she herself has never seen.

Memories are wildly percolating within me. My mind goes back to a tour I took of the Palace in June 1989, six months before the Revolution. The complex, a construction site in those days, was completely surrounded by an eight-foot fence, an attempt to keep citizens of Bucharest from knowing the full extent of the sinfully extravagant, outlandish structure being built while displaced citizens and home-owners suffered and died from starvation and exposure.

As I thank the guide for her tour when she returns us to the security point, I tell her that perhaps I've seen more of the Palace than she ever has, places like the floors belowground.

Her face turns white. I explain that in 1989 several construction workers took me and another Western woman on a tour of the site. All it took, on a cloudy day in June, to get the attention of a guard through a large crack in the eight-foot fence was a loud, "Psst! Psst!" Through the crack we negotiated his price to take us on a tour of the place. He calmly suggested a bag of coffee.[125] When we returned with the bag, the guard told us to meet at a less obvious hole in the fence further down the street. Once inside the grounds, the guard and his buddy gave us an extensive tour of the closely guarded palace. One would run ahead to make sure it was safe to go further,

---

124 In the main theatre, we were shown a chandelier so large that four men could crawl around inside to clean it. The guide mentioned casually that no one wants to sit underneath the chandelier in case it falls on them during a performance.

125 In the eighties, Romanian currency was worthless. People used coffee to get what they needed. A one-pound bag of coffee was worth sixty dollars on the street, but it was available only to tourists for a few dollars at Dollar Shops in large hotels. Coffee was used by Romanians in exchange for services—for example, to barter for the safe delivery of a child in one of the country's deplorable hospitals. It was the most meaningful "currency" in a country where the Romanian *leu* had no value.

opening the doors for us to see into the rooms and closing them behind us as we moved through the building. Oh, the foolishness naiveté of youth!

I'm back on the streets of this city that never sleeps, sitting now at a trendy sidewalk cafe in Centru Vechi (Old Town), a creamy latte in my hands. Nearby, I hear the staccato of hammers, the scream of saws, and voices of builders bent on transforming an old building (that looks like it may fall down at any moment) into something new. In my reverie, I think of the words voiced in 1990 by Silviu Brucan, one of Romania's communist revolutionaries who opposed Ceausescu—that it would take Romania a generation to move beyond the ravages of the Ceausescu years. His words are only partially true.[126] Not just one but *several* generations have passed.

I ask myself if this broken city is still in the process of rebirth, as the monument on Revolution Square, the Memorial of Rebirth, suggests. But what is the role of remembering when so much brokenness remains to be healed? Nobody talks about communism today. How can they remember or understand the ashes from which rebirth will happen if they have never heard the stories?

In the future, when your children ask you, "What do these stones mean?" tell them that the flow of the Jordan was cut off before the ark of the covenant of the Lord. When it crossed the Jordan, the waters of the Jordan were cut off. These stones are to be a memorial to the people of Israel forever... He did this so that all the peoples of the earth might know that the hand of the Lord is powerful and so that you might always fear the Lord your God.

—Joshua 4:6–7, 24

---

126 Associated Press, "Silviu Brucan, 90, Opponent of Ceausescu, Dies," *The New York Times*, September 16, 2006 (https://www.nytimes.com/2006/09/16/world/europe/16brucan.html).

Appendix

A BRIEF HISTORY OF BEE (BIBLICAL EDUCATION BY EXTENSION)

Biblical Education by Extension (BEE) began in the early eighties as a partnership among Christian mission organizations and interested individuals, all of whom had already been involved with the underground church. Until then, groups had engaged in one-on-one discipleship, compassion ministries, and the smuggling of literature to Central and Eastern Europe and Russia. By the end of the seventies, only small pockets of pastoral education had been developed for church leaders in these countries; seminaries had been closed by communist regimes. A new generation of pastors served with little biblical or pastoral education.

At a historic meeting in Vienna, Austria in 1979, a small collaborative group of three mission organizations recognized the need for pastoral education across Eastern Europe and Russia. The development and leadership of a newly envisioned program was eventually delegated to two visionaries who understood the components of non-traditional theological and pastoral education. Their names were Jody Dillow and Al Bridges. After the meeting in 1979 with only a handful of agencies and interested individuals, twelve missions eventually joined BEE. In 1983, Jody and Al invited me to join the project, though whether pastors in Eastern Europe would be open to women teaching in the program had not been brought up, much less approved.

A comprehensive biblical training program was launched in the early eighties with on-the-ground headquarters in Vienna. Offices were also established in the USA, where charitable donations for the ambitious project could be processed. In these offices, the selection, writing, and translation of curriculum into multiple Eastern European languages began, and facilitators for the discipleship model of education in Eastern Europe were recruited.

The vision behind the quickly growing ministry, operating out of an old three-storey house in Vienna, was to train Eastern European pastors who served multiple churches, often with little or no pastoral training. There were no faculty, only a team of men who travelled into Eastern Europe as facilitators, usually on tourist visas, teaching for weeks or months at a time with small groups of pastors in hidden places across these countries.

The heart of the ministry was a multiplication model based on Paul's instructions to Timothy, his son in the faith, in 2 Timothy 2:2: *"And the things you have heard me say in the presence of many witnesses entrust to reliable people who will also be qualified to teach others."* Embedded in Paul's model was the concept of one generation teaching the next, who in turn would gather around themselves yet another generation. It was a model that worked in repressive contexts where schools couldn't be built and curriculum had to be smuggled to those who would use it. It was a model of multiplication that had in view exponential growth in the number of persons trained. At the time I was recruited for the BEE project in 1982, it was attractive to me for three reasons:

1) The Size of the Vision: BEE, in its early days, was spoken of as one of the most ambitious projects of theological curriculum development in the history of the church. The curriculum was written, translated, printed, and then delivered by Bible smugglers to small groups across Eastern Europe. Initially, a handful of foundational courses were developed in six or seven Eastern European languages for delivery in countries where Christian literature was contraband. The project was God-sized.

2) The Non-Formal Educational Plan: BEE was ahead of its time. It focused on the delivery of pastoral education in non-formal ways to contexts where formal theological education in residential schools with established faculties was prohibited by communist governments. Formal Bible schools and seminaries had been closed or severely decreased in size so as to be almost insignificant. The project depended on non-formal methods of education.

3) The Partnership in Mission: BEE was a collaborative effort of mission groups in a project so ambitious and ahead of its time that it was mind-boggling, even by today's standards. Participants from a number of established mission groups believed they could be more effective working together with other like-minded groups than on their own. In the mission world of those days, partnership and collaboration was a new and exciting venture, especially at such a level.

When I began exploring the possibility of joining BEE in 1982, I was impressed that such a large number of international workers could work together, seldom mentioning the mission group that supported them. The old house in the eighteenth district of Vienna housed curriculum writers, design artists, administrators, technology technicians, fundraisers, and facilitators who made their home in Austria and travelled to different Eastern European countries to facilitate small groups of pastors. These IWs delighted in a warm, collaborative community that served the pastors of Eastern Europe and Russia. What united this amazing group of people—Americans, Canadians, Europeans, South Americans, and Asians—was the vision of bringing quality pastoral education to pastors and leaders in Eastern Europe.

After the revolutions of 1989, the Iron Curtain and the Berlin Wall were dismantled. The delivery of pastoral education with the cloak and dagger intrigue that had been characteristic of the eighties was no longer necessary. National churches that had received BEE facilitators and curriculum for ten years began to take responsibility for the development of biblical and pastoral education that was contextually and culturally appropriate in their country. Repeatedly, we heard that in the post-Revolution world, Eastern European churches recognized a foundation upon which to build as they began to develop Christian colleges, seminaries, and mission-sending agencies across Eastern and Central Europe.

Training for Women

Following a fact-finding trip in late 1983 (see Chapter 1), I was invited by Jody Dillow and Al Bridges to explore a program for women parallel to the pastoral training program that was already flourishing among men across Eastern Europe. That is the story of this book. God in his goodness brought many women to Vienna to join the Women's Ministries team.

Among the first to join as full-time facilitators were two faithful women, Doreen Mellot and Wendy Wilson. Later, Lorraine Schukar, Debbie Skufka, Paula Tipton, and Liz Loeffler joined. Wives of the men who travelled from Vienna as facilitators joined as part-time travellers. Some of those who come to mind are Myrna Alexander, Diane Bible, Linda Bridges, Sherry Bohn, Linda Dillow, Claire Gibson, Mary Ginter, Mary Keppeler, Valinda Kimmel, Carol Klingsmith, Arlis Mitchell, Virginia Moreira, Charlotte Olson, Nancy Peterson, Sandy Shaffer and Lou Ann Temple. The women's ministry of BEE adopted the same educational model and non-formal delivery plan, looking to 2 Timothy 2:2 for its design.

Before long, Romanian pastors pointed to the growth of their wives as a result of their involvement in the training program. They acknowledged that their own ministry was enhanced because their wives were growing as leaders, and their wives understood in new ways what it meant for their husbands to be in ministry.

When the Iron Curtain came down in 1989, God took the founding vision of Biblical Education by Extension and scattered the ministry around the world through the formation of two effective successor ministries: BEE World (https://www.beeworld.org/) and Entrust (BEE International; https://www.entrust4.org/). Both organizations look to the same historical roots, dating back to 1979. In

2019, both groups celebrated forty years of God's faithfulness. They continue today to invest in the leaders of the next generation in hard places.

Afterword

When the Apollo 13 moon landing ran into trouble and the mission had to be aborted, a key player turned out to be Ken, an astronaut who was supposed to have been on the Apollo mission, but couldn't go because of health concerns. To prevent his colleagues from literally being lost forever in outer space, Ken got into a simulator at the mission control centre in Houston, working almost twelve hours at a stretch to develop a re-entry strategy.

At one point in the movie, *Apollo 13*, the mission commander asked Ken, "Do you need a break?" I will never forget Ken's response. It sent the proverbial shivers down my spine when I heard it. He responded, "If they don't get a break, I don't."

Immediately my mind went to the many international workers from our church who were lost—not in the outer darkness of space, but in its spiritual equivalent, seeking to bring home the lost among the nations. I was convicted afresh that we, the "senders," need to take our place in the simulator—praying, giving, refreshing, and encouraging the "goers"—as active partners with the same mentality: "If they don't get a break, I don't!"

Miriam Charter's book, an exquisite combination of theology and practice, concept and story, joy and sorrow, local and global, individual and corporate, is a worthy companion for any pastor who wants to fulfil his calling to build a global impact church, one who refuses to take a break from his global engagement because "if they don't get a break, I don't!"

—Sunder Krishnan
Pastor of Rexdale Alliance Church (Etobicoke, ON)
for thirty-six years (retired)
author of *Hijacked by Glory: From the Pew to the Nations* (2014)

Glossary

Apparatchik: Historically, the name given to a member of the Communist Party who had managerial responsibilities that didn't require much competence; a somewhat negative title.

Atheism; atheist: Lack of belief in deities; a person who holds no belief in a deity or deities.

Berlin Wall: A guarded concrete barrier that divided Berlin both physically and psychologically from 1961 to 1989.

To bug (verb); bug (noun): The practice of concealing a miniature microphone in a room or telephone in order to monitor or record a conversation; the "bug" refers to the tiny microphone.

Cold War: The ongoing political rivalry between the USA and the Soviet Union and their respective allies that developed after World War II and continued until the breakup of the Soviet Union (roughly 1947–1991).

Culture: An integrated system of beliefs, values, artifacts, and customs which bind a society together and give it a sense of identity, dignity, security, and continuity. At the heart of culture is its worldview, answering the most basic question, "What is real?"[127]

Creative Access Nation: A country that may not allow missionary work; creative means are needed to gain entry for mission. Sometimes referred to as a Limited Access Nation.

Diaspora: A scattered population that originates from a different geographic location. Historically, the word referred to the involuntary spread of people from their original homeland, as in the *Jewish diaspora*.

Eastern Bloc: The group of communist states in Central and Eastern Europe, East and Southeast Asia that collaborated under the leadership of the Soviet Union from 1947–1991; also known as the Communist Bloc.

---

127 *Kairos, God, the Church and the World* (Living Springs International, 2011), p. ii.

General revelation: General truths that can be known about God as revealed through nature.

Gypsy: An Indo-Aryan nomadic people group, living primarily in Europe but increasingly in the Americas; believed to have originated from south Asia. Thirty years ago they were called "gypsies" (*ţigani*) but today, "gypsy" may be considered by some a racist label; now called (officially) "Roma" because of their Romany language, though in Romania many still prefer to call themselves gypsy (*ţigan*). In this book, both terms are used depending on the era referred to.

Indoctrination: Teaching or forcing a person or group to accept beliefs uncritically.

International worker: Persons living and working abroad (excluding tourists and transients); includes workers, businesspeople, entrepreneurs, students, mission workers, and others who live and work in an international context; in this book also referred to as IWs.

Iron Curtain: For thirty-eight years, from the end of World War II up to the end of the Cold War, a symbolic (in places, physical) boundary line that divided Europe into two political regions; a barrier to the free flow of mission work into Eastern and Central Europe and Russia; included the Berlin Wall and many kilometres of barbed wire fence as its physical expression.

Lei/leu: The currency of Romania prior to the Euro; *leu* is singular; *lei* is plural.

Limited Access Nation: Countries to which missions and missionaries are not given easy access or permission to openly spread the gospel; see also Creative Access Nation.

Maoism: A variation of Marxism-Leninism that Mao Zedong developed in bringing about a socialist revolution in the People's Republic of China.

Missional (missiology): Used to describe churches and people who intentionally participate in the *missio Dei* (mission of God); implies the adopting of thinking and behaviours that will help to engage others with the gospel message; related terms are missiology (the discipline or study of mission) and missiologist (a person who specializes in the discipline of missiology).

Nation: Biblically, an ethnic unit or group of people having its own language, customs and culture; in Greek the word is *ethnos;* not a politically defined country, but similar to people group.

People group: A group of individuals who see themselves as having a common affinity for each other because of their shared language, religion, ethnicity, caste, etc. or a combination of any of these.[128]

Roma: See Gypsy.

---

128 Ibid., p. iii.

Scientific atheism: The main goal of Marxist-Leninist scientific atheism is to discover and assimilate "scientific" data and use it to destroy religion and any belief in deities. Using data primarily from the natural sciences, it attempts to demonstrate the non-existence of God.

Secret police/Securitate: Police or intelligence agencies that engage in covert operations against opponents of an authoritarian regime. The Securitate was the secret police of the Socialist Republic of Romania; terms used interchangeably in this book.

Seminary: A graduate educational institution that prepares clergy or people training for Christian ministry; follows after an undergraduate program; includes studies in Scripture, theology, church history, and the practice of serving the church.

Special revelation: God's revelation of himself through miraculous means, the ultimate miracle being the person of Jesus (John calls him the Word made flesh). The Bible, God's Word, is also special revelation, as are dreams, visions, and physical appearances of God.

Systematization: A twentieth-century program of rural resettlement under Ceausescu to transform Romania's agricultural economy to an industrial one. Villages and historic buildings were demolished and villagers relocated to cities.

Underground church/underground: A term used during the Cold War in communist states and today in totalitarian and radical Islamic states to refer to churches that do not fully submit to the authority of the state. Though church buildings may be visible on the street and leaders are known to the state, the real life of the Body is found in that which happens in secret, hidden from the view of everyday citizens; hence, referred to as "underground."

Unreached People Group (UPG): A group that currently has little access to the gospel; there is no possibility, given current conditions, that they can hear the gospel in their own language in a way that makes sense to them. UPGs don't have enough followers of Jesus or the resources required to evangelize their own people, so they need help from the outside to do so; used interchangeably with Least Reached People Group.

About the Author

Miriam Charter is a mission practitioner, speaker, and mobilizer based in Calgary. She spent ten years as an international worker in communist Europe working among women in the underground church, and several years in post-communist Russia learning Russian and doing research on post-communist societies. Her doctoral studies focused on theological education for the emerging church in post-communist societies.

Miriam has a pronounced calling to the nations. This calling was due in part to her multi-cultural, international background: born in China to missionary parents, raised in Canada, a French teacher by profession, an international worker in France, Central and Eastern Europe (primarily Romania, Bulgaria, Hungary, and Czechoslovakia), and several years in post-communist Russia. She has three primary passions:

1. Those who, through no fault of their own, have never heard of Jesus.
2. Those who suffer today because they are willing to be known as followers of Jesus.
3. The next generation of international workers who will receive the baton passed to them and take the Good News to the nations. Nothing brings her greater delight than mentoring young adults and speaking into the life of anyone willing to explore God's call to mission.

The story of her call to mission through the local church is a message she loves to share. Her strong belief in the model of 2 Timothy 2:2—one generation teaching the next generation, which in turn will teach others—is another of her stories, told in this book and whenever she speaks.

Miriam's academic and teaching career was divided between Trinity Evangelical Divinity School (Deerfield, IL) and Ambrose University and Seminary (Calgary, AB). She has a B.Ed. (French) from the University of Calgary, an M.Div. from reGeneration

Ambrose Seminary, and a Ph.D. from Trinity Evangelical Divinity School. She continues to champion the local church, loving her involvements at Foothills Alliance Church with the Global Impact Team and teaching Alpha and ESL to newcomers to Canada in the International Ministries department.

To contact Miriam, visit her website or send an email to:

www.reGenerationBook.ca
regenerationbook@gmail.com